DOCTOR DW WHO
THE VISUAL DICTIONARY

Acute senses

Latest sonic screwdriver model

Trademark bow tie

Time Lord physiognomy

Two hearts

Time Lords originate from the planet Gallifrey

907 years old

Doctor's Eleventh body

THE ELEVENTH DOCTOR

Secondary
Stun barrel

Powercell

NOVICE HAME'S GUN

Carbonised shell

Capable of
exploding an entire
spacestation

WARP STAR

Amelia's
representation
of the Doctor

Clothes raggedy
from TARDIS
explosion

DOLL OF THE DOCTOR

Saturnyne blood
transfused into
human veins

Blood transforms
cellular structure
from human to
Saturnyne

Map of the
company's complex

Vouchers for the
office canteen

OOD OPERATIONS PRESS PACK

Enhanced targeting gear

Stun ray
muzzle

FREEDOM FIGHTER GUN

Clear fluid
reduces risk of
death through
dehydration

Cuffs restrain
victim during
transfusion

SATURNYNE
CHAIR

Holds pupils of the
House of Calvierri

RETROFITTED BETAMAX
VIDEO RECORDER

Fits in a small handbag

RIVER SONG'S PISTOL

DETONATOR PACK

Flashes red
when primed

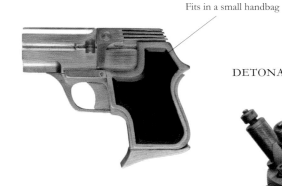

Base attaches
to any surface

Perfectly
moulded to face

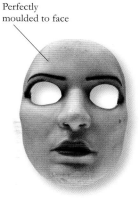

LIZ TEN'S
MASK

DOCTOR DW WHO
BBC

THE VISUAL DICTIONARY

Written by NEIL CORRY, JACQUELINE RAYNER, ANDREW DARLING,
KERRIE DOUGHERTY, DAVID JOHN and SIMON BEECROFT

Frazzled by too
much power
attracting the
Atraxi

SONIC SCREWDRIVER

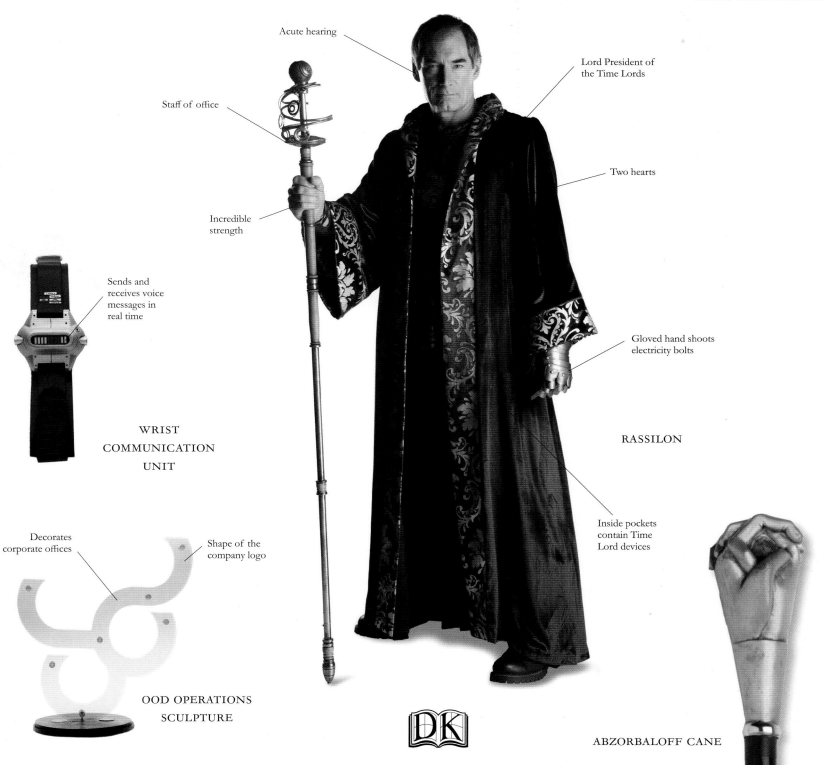

Acute hearing

Staff of office

Incredible
strength

Lord President of
the Time Lords

Two hearts

Gloved hand shoots
electricity bolts

RASSILON

Inside pockets
contain Time
Lord devices

Sends and
receives voice
messages in
real time

WRIST
COMMUNICATION
UNIT

Decorates
corporate offices

Shape of the
company logo

OOD OPERATIONS
SCULPTURE

ABZORBALOFF CANE

DK

Contents

6 Mysterious Visitor

8 The Time Lord

10 Anatomy of the Doctor

12 Regeneration

14 The TARDIS

20 Sonic Screwdrivers

22 Tools of the Trade

24 Amy Pond

26 Rory Williams

28 Leadworth

30 River Song

32 Captain Jack Harkness

33 Donna Noble

34 Rose Tyler

35 Martha Jones

36 Torchwood

37 UNIT

38 Sarah Jane Smith

39 K-9

40 John Smith

42 Daleks

44 Dalek Flagship

46 The Genesis Ark

48 Doomsday Ghosts

50 The Cult of Skaro

52 Dalek Sec

54 Davros

56 Davros's Empire

58 Ironsides

60 The New Daleks

62 Weeping Angels

64 Army of Angels

66 The Ood

68 Cybermen

70 Cybus Industries

72 The CyberKing

74 Platform One

76 Guests of *Platform One*

77 Lady Cassandra

78 The Slitheen

80 Satellite 5

82 The Sycorax

84 New Earth

86 The Werewolf

88 The Gelth

89 Krillitanes

90 SS *Madame de Pompadour*

92 The Beast

94 Racnoss

95 Plasmavores

96 The Judoon

98 Carrionites

100 The Family of Blood

102 The Master

104 The Toclafane

106 The Master Race

108 Time Lords

110 The Heavenly Host

112 Adipose Industries

113 Vespiform

114 Pyroviles

116 Sontaran

118 The Hath

120 Vashta Nerada

121 The Flood

122 San Helios

124 Prisoner Zero

126 Smilers

128 Star Whale

130 Saturnyns

132 Silurians

134 Silurian Warriors

136 The Pandorica

138 Enemies

140 Time Energy

142 Index

Mysterious Visitor

TIME AND TIME AGAIN, fate seems to thrust a mysterious time traveller known as the Doctor into the right place at the right time. However, because the Doctor always arrives at times of catastrophe, some legends have evolved that suggest he is the cause of these events. In fact, he is usually instrumental in the resolution of crises, but like a storm, he can also leave damage in his wake. The Doctor was a crucial figure in the Great Time War between the Daleks and the Time Lords in which, for the sake of the universe, he was driven to bring out the destruction of the Daleks, the Time Lords and his home planet, Gallifrey. The Doctor continues to appear where he is needed to alleviate the chaos created in both time and space.

THE DOCTOR

Target: Earth

Many alien races have sought to invade the Earth, to enslave humanity, rob it of its mineral wealth or simply destroy the planet. Displaced beings such as the Nestene Consciousness, the Gelth and the Saturnyns have sought refuge on Earth, while the Daleks have made it the focus of many attacks, once even towing it to another galaxy. A megalomaniac Time Lord known as the Master has twice tried to conquer Earth and make it a battleship to wage war on the universe. Fortunately for humanity the Doctor has often defeated these plans and saved the world.

England, and London in particular, have seen more than a few attempts at alien invasion. However, few citizens of the 20th or 21st centuries would be aware of them, thanks to the efforts of UNIT and the Torchwood Institute, Earth-based organisations who defeat and cover up alien threats.

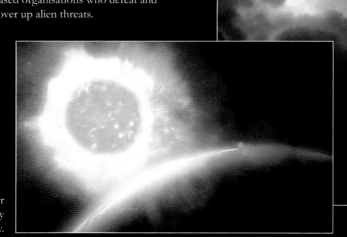

The Earth eventually dies in the year 5.5/Apple/26. It is destroyed naturally by the expanding Sun, not by an enemy.

The Super Highway

The Doctor travels in a TARDIS – an advanced piece of Time Lord technology that can time travel. His Type 40 ship looks like a 1960s police box. TARDISes move from one moment or place to another by passing through the time vortex: a swirling mass of energy that links all points in time and space.

The Time Lord

THE DOCTOR believes himself to be the last surviving Time Lord – a long-lived and incredibly technologically advanced race, which possessed the secret of time travel. The Time Lords preferred to observe the universe and rarely interfered in the affairs of other worlds, whereas the Doctor has a strong sense of right and wrong, and a firm conviction that he should intervene to prevent injustice. Unable to agree with a policy of non-intervention, the Doctor became a "renegade", stealing a TARDIS and using it to explore time and space.

There is Only One Doctor

When Time Lords come to the end of their lives, they have the ability to regenerate their bodies and carry on living. Although each regeneration brings out different facets of a Time Lord's personality, the Doctor's essential character has remained unchanged for centuries. His affable and child-like traits conceal an extensive knowledge of the universe and deep wisdom born of experience.

Every time the Doctor regenerates, he selects an outfit to suit his new personality. The Eleventh Doctor is not afraid to have fun with his quirky style.

The TARDIS

Mythical Hero

The Doctor's appearances on Earth and services to humanity have gone down in legend and references to him are scattered throughout folklore. The "Man in the Blue Box" takes on an almost religious significance in this stained glass window from a London church in 2010.

Clothes are non-threatening

The Doctor has a gift for appearing at critical moments in time when catastrophe is about to strike, including the launch of the *Titanic* and at the eruption of Krakatoa.

Travelling Through Time

The gift of time travel also brings responsibility. The rules of time are fluid and complicated. Actions have consequences and not all time is in flux – some tragedies cannot be reversed.

Maintaining Time

The Doctor has prevented catastrophe from rewriting the future of Earth many times. He sees his relationship with humans as a strength, but his enemies regard it as a weakness that is easy to exploit. By threatening Earth during World War II, the Daleks know that Winston Churchill will call his good friend the Doctor, who walks straight into the trap.

Missed Opportunities

Some moments are temporal tipping points, where decisive action could create a new timeline. When the future pivots around human-Silurian negotiations for a cohabitation deal, the Doctor is hopeful for a new era of Earth. Sadly, talks break down, the Silurians return to hibernation and life on Earth continues as before.

No Room for Manoeuvre

Some events are fixed and cannot be changed. The Doctor can only mourn and carry on. On Bowie Base One, the Doctor refuses to follow the rules of time and rescues the crew. But base leader, Adelaide Brooke, was destined to die to ensure a good future. She does what the Doctor could not and kills herself.

Man's Best Friend

The Doctor feels a special affinity for the human race. Even though he has witnessed the very worst of human behaviour, he is still awed by their potential for goodness. He cannot bear to stand by and watch humanity suffer – especially if children are crying.

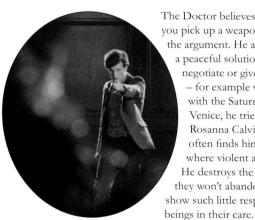

The Doctor believes that the moment you pick up a weapon, you have lost the argument. He always looks for a peaceful solution first, trying to negotiate or give aliens a choice – for example when confronted with the Saturnyns' plan to sink Venice, he tries to reason with Rosanna Calvierri. However, he often finds himself in situations where violent action is necessary. He destroys the Saturnyns because they won't abandon their plan and they show such little respect for the human beings in their care.

Despite his vibrant personality, the Doctor is sometimes overwhelmed by his belief that he is the last surviving Time Lord. He has developed strong relationships with many humans, but they are limited because of his extraordinary longevity and the fact that his life is fraught with danger. He leads a solitary life, punctuated by the company of people who travel with him, but who must always return to their own lives.

Doctor Facts

• The Doctor's body temperature is a cool 59-61 degrees Fahrenheit (15-16 Celsius), lower than the typical human body temperature of 98.6 degrees Fahrenheit (37 Celsius).

• This Time Lord is qualified in "practically everything," but has never actually received a medical degree.

• He was a member of a Time Lord clan called the Prydon Chapter. The Prydonians were said to be the most powerful and devious of all the Chapters.

• At the Prydon Academy, the young Doctor just scraped through with a 51 per cent pass, and it was on his second attempt.

• River Song may be the only non-Gallifreyan to know the Doctor's real name, although the Doctor claims that it is unpronounceable for humans. His nickname at the Prydon Academy was "Theta Sigma".

• Queen Victoria once knighted the Doctor under the name "Sir Doctor of TARDIS".

• The Doctor had a brother and a granddaughter, Susan, but lost his entire family long ago. More recently, he acquired a biological "daughter," Jenny, grown from a tissue sample on the planet Messaline.

Anatomy of the Doctor

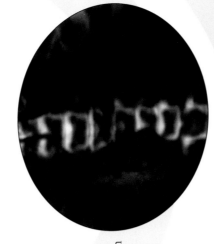

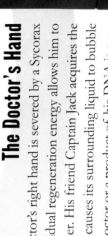

Nutrient fluid preserves severed hand

ALTHOUGH HE LOOKS LIKE a human being (and once claimed human ancestry on his mother's side), the Doctor is an alien being and his Time Lord physiology has many differences to our own. Physically, the Doctor is stronger, has sharper senses and greater powers of endurance than a human being and can cope with heat, cold, radiation and strange energies better than humans can. There are also some differences to his internal anatomy that have confused many Earthly doctors.

Two Hearts

Time Lords have two hearts and a binary vascular system, which enables them to survive major accidents and many physical and temporal shocks that would kill a human being. They also have a respiratory by-pass system that enables them to survive without breathing for some time.

Time Lord life-energy is tremendously vibrant and powerful. When the TARDIS's power supply is almost totally destroyed, save for one cell, the Tenth Doctor recharges it by breathing his own life energy into the remaining power cell, giving up 10 years of his life in the process.

The Doctor's Hand

When the Doctor's right hand is severed by a Sycorax warrior, residual regeneration energy allows him to grow another. His friend Captain Jack acquires the original, which causes its surrounding liquid to bubble whenever the Doctor or a product of his DNA is near.

Highly developed Time Lord brain, with great memory capacity and telepathic ability

Highly evolved senses – he can identify blood groups by taste and pinpoint historical eras by smell

Respiratory by-pass system allows short-term survival in airless environments

Lower body temperature than a human

Eye colour – like all physical features – can change with regeneration

Two hearts, supported by a binary vascular system

Superhuman strength and stamina

Two Doctors

A biological metacrisis combines genetic information from the Doctor's severed hand and from the human Donna Noble, with energy from an abortive regeneration, to grow a new Doctor, who is half-Time Lord/half-human. Although he looks like the Tenth Doctor, he has one heart and is unable to regenerate.

A smarter version of the Doctor's clothes

A Darker Side

Physically the Doctor is stronger than any human, but psychologically he is just as vulnerable. And with the life he's had, he's seen more dark things than any human. When psychic pollen gets into the TARDIS machinery, it induces a dream state for the Doctor, Amy and Rory. It feeds on the Doctor's fears and insecurities, giving them a voice in the form of the Dream Lord. This malign manifestation taunts the Doctor and revels in playing games of life and death with him and his friends.

Another Time Lord, the Master, temporarily suspends the Doctor's capacity to regenerate. Without this, his body would be over 900 years old, so he becomes a tiny wizened creature as he reaches his full age.

Miniature version of the Tenth Doctor's clothes

Body can absorb Röntgen radiation, endure massive gamma radiation strikes and survive cyanide poisoning

Assuming that the Doctor is human, the Silurians begin a decontamination process on him to neutralise harmful bacteria and viruses in his system. Screaming in agony, the Doctor points out that he is a Time Lord and those human germs are keeping him alive.

The Doctor's clothes help him appear non-threatening

Comfortable shoes for a quick escape and a lot of running

Regeneration

IN CASES OF ADVANCED age, mortal illness or fatal injury, Time Lords have the ability to regenerate their bodies to create a new physical form. There is a notable shift in personality too, due to chemical changes in the brain. The regeneration process takes many hours. It is hugely traumatic and can cause mental and psychological instability until it is completed.

Four Knocks

A psychic named Carmen tells the Doctor that, "your song is ending... he will knock four times" but she doesn't reveal who "he" is. To the Doctor's surprise, the man who knocks four times is not a great enemy, but a man who could not respect and love him more: Wilfred Mott.

Knowing that the end is close, the Doctor has the chance to say his goodbyes. He attends Donna's wedding from a safe distance and returns to see his old friends: he visits a younger Rose Tyler, rescues Martha from a Sontaran, sets Captain Jack up with a date and saves Sarah Jane's son from a car accident.

Tenth Doctor

Amid the havoc of the invasion of the Master and the Time Lord High Council, Donna's grandfather, Wilfred Mott, becomes trapped inside a radiation chamber. Wilf knocks on the glass door four times to get the Doctor's attention. Wilf is willing to die, but the Doctor chooses to save him and absorbs a fatal dose of radiation which begins the regeneration process. Although he accepts the inevitability of regeneration, the Tenth Doctor does not yet feel ready to go.

As cellular restructure begins, the Doctor's body starts to glow with regeneration energy.

The process of regeneration is much like dying because a Time Lord loses so much, even though it is the same Time Lord who comes back. It is a terrifying experience because the outcome is unknown.

A Devastating Change

Unlike previous regenerations inside the TARDIS, when the Tenth Doctor regenerates it creates havoc in the spacecraft. Possibly because of the incredible amount of radiation he's absorbed, the Doctor's regeneration energy shoots out from his body with such force that it causes the console to explode, setting off a chain reaction.

The TARDIS windows are blown out by the phenomenal power of the Doctor's regeneration.

It's unusual for the Doctor to regenerate alone, but it's lucky in the Tenth Doctor's case – it's doubtful anyone else would have survived the destruction his change causes.

Comforting Words

The telepathic Ood can see the Tenth Doctor's death is coming. In gratitude for his rescuing them in the past, they sing to the Doctor to soothe his transition and give him strength for the agonising process.

A new body requires a period of readjustment. Confusion, erratic behaviour and memory loss are common. When the Eleventh Doctor meets Amelia he is consumed with new cravings. After trying and discarding an apple, fried bacon, yoghurt, beans, and bread and butter, his new taste buds are finally satisfied with fish fingers dipped in custard.

Eleventh Doctor

Although there's a new face in the TARDIS, the latest version of the Doctor is still the bravest man in the universe. He uses brain over brawn, proudly defends Earth, lives life with a passion and never hides his anger when he sees the suffering of others. The Eleventh Doctor is still the man monsters have nightmares about.

The new Doctor is upset he isn't ginger

The Eleventh Doctor loves human fashions, particularly bow ties

Eleven Faces – One Time Lord

Time Lords can have 13 lives before their bodies are unable to regenerate again but it has been suggested that an entirely new regeneration cycle can be started, presumably by artificial means.

The First Doctor changes after defeating a Cyberman invasion.

The Time Lords transform the Second Doctor's appearance.

The Third Doctor dies while fighting the Great One.

The Fourth Doctor gives his life to stop the evil Master.

The Fifth Doctor's worries that he won't regenerate after being poisoned are not founded.

The Sixth Doctor is badly injured when the TARDIS is attacked.

The Seventh Doctor dies in surgery due to an unsuitable anaesthetic.

No one knows the cause of the Eighth Doctor's regeneration.

Saving Rose from vortex energy causes the Ninth Doctor's change.

Rescuing Wilf causes the Tenth Doctor to be fatally poisoned by radiation.

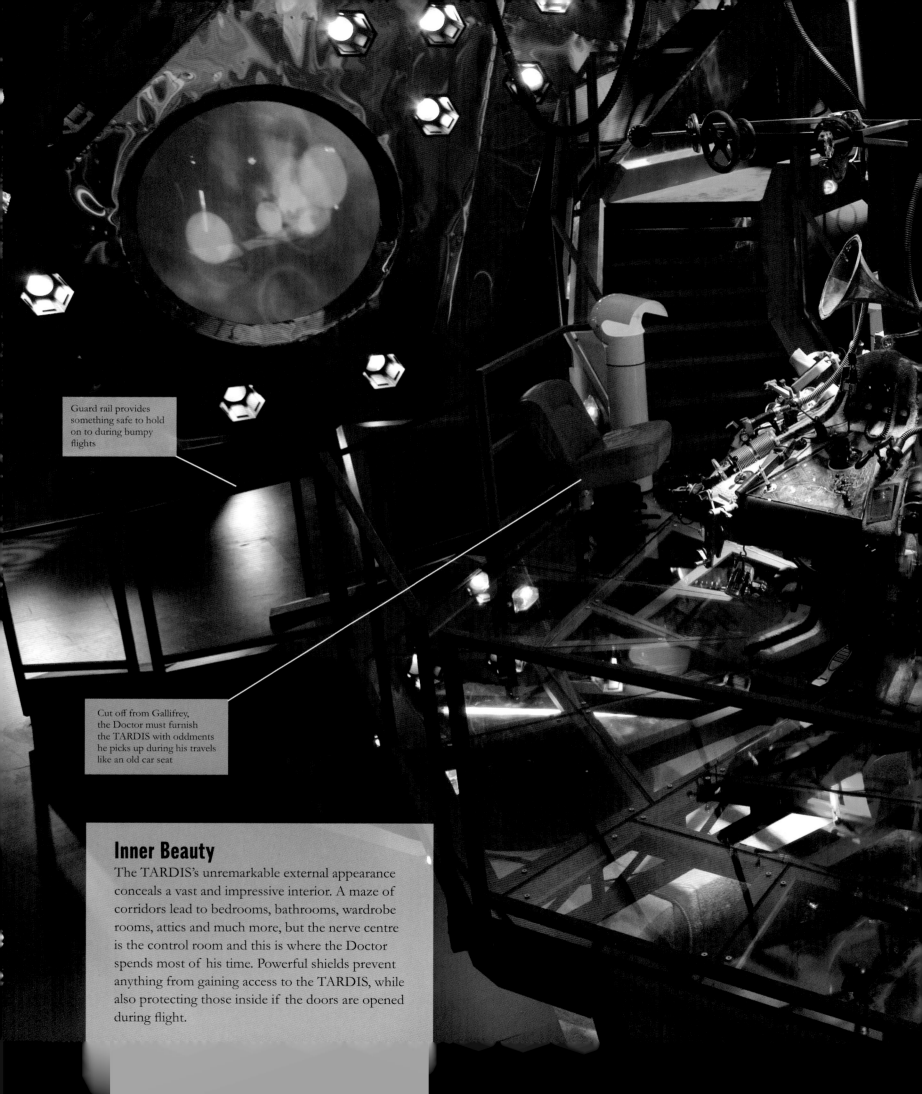

Guard rail provides something safe to hold on to during bumpy flights

Cut off from Gallifrey, the Doctor must furnish the TARDIS with oddments he picks up during his travels like an old car seat

Inner Beauty

The TARDIS's unremarkable external appearance conceals a vast and impressive interior. A maze of corridors lead to bedrooms, bathrooms, wardrobe rooms, attics and much more, but the nerve centre is the control room and this is where the Doctor spends most of his time. Powerful shields prevent anything from gaining access to the TARDIS, while also protecting those inside if the doors are opened during flight.

Inside the TARDIS

TIME LORD TIME-SPACE engineering allows the TARDIS to be significantly larger on the inside than on the outside. Because the TARDIS is dimensionally transcendental, its interior and exterior exist in different dimensions and are connected by a space-time bridge at the TARDIS's entrance. The interior can be configured in almost any way the TARDIS's pilot wishes.

TARDIS Power

The TARDIS's space-time travel is fuelled by a temporal energy called Artron energy, generated both by the Eye of Harmony (an artificial black hole on Gallifrey) and by Time Lords' minds. Artron energy from the Eye was transferred to a miniature copy of the Eye and stored in the TARDIS console. When Rose looks into the open TARDIS console she gazes into the heart of this energy and can see all time at once.

A chameleon circuit allows TARDISes to blend in with their surroundings, but the Doctor's TARDIS got stuck as a police box on a visit to 1960s London. It now looks out of place almost everywhere, especially in ancient Pompeii, but a perception filter means most people pay it little attention.

Freezing Cold

When psychic pollen gets into the time rotor, a manifestation of the Doctor's psyche – the Dream Lord – appears to set the TARDIS on course for a cold sun that could freeze everything to death.

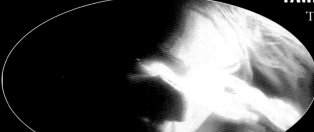

Famous Visitors

The usual response from astonished visitors to the TARDIS is, "It's bigger on the inside than the outside". But artist Vincent van Gogh sees things differently from most people. His first comment is about the colour scheme – he likes it.

Grown to Size

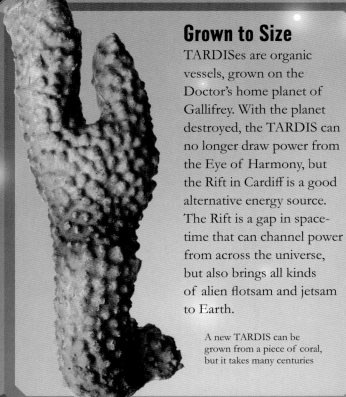

TARDISes are organic vessels, grown on the Doctor's home planet of Gallifrey. With the planet destroyed, the TARDIS can no longer draw power from the Eye of Harmony, but the Rift in Cardiff is a good alternative energy source. The Rift is a gap in space-time that can channel power from across the universe, but also brings all kinds of alien flotsam and jetsam to Earth.

A new TARDIS can be grown from a piece of coral, but it takes many centuries

Tardy

Running in a newly configured TARDIS is not a smooth process. The Doctor intends to return to Amelia after five minutes, but a blip makes him 12 years late and she's all grown up.

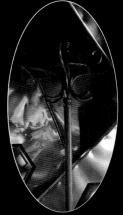

Among the many customised rooms are an immense wardrobe, a cinema, a swimming pool, a library and a garage.

Spare TARDIS
key concealed
behind "P"

Phone concealed
behind panel is
non-functional, as
it is not connected
to telephone lines

More Powerful than a Black Hole

The Time Lords artificially created a black hole
called the Eye of Harmony. The captured energy
of this black hole is the source of the TARDIS's
power and is so strong
that the TARDIS can
escape from the
gravitational pull of
another black hole.
The Doctor uses this
tremendous power
to tow Earth back to
its rightful position,
after it is moved to
the Medusa Cascade
by the Daleks.

The TARDIS
can be unlocked
by a key, by remote
systems and even
with the snap of
the Doctor's fingers

A St. John
Ambulance badge
reflects the use of
old police boxes as
a point of first aid

Sonic Screwdrivers

THE STANDARD TOOLKIT in a TARDIS contains equipment needed to tune and repair the ship. One of the most useful tools, the sonic screwdriver, uses variously focused soundwaves to make repairs where human hands cannot reach. As well as turning screws, it can open locks, operate and repair ship systems remotely, and take many kinds of readings and scans.

Although the Doctor gets a new sonic screwdriver, it still can't break deadlock seals, work on wood or override the protocols on the *Byzantium* ship, which are being controlled by the Weeping Angels.

Time Technology

Sonic screwdrivers are a common Time Lord device. In fact, the Doctor has a number of them onboard the TARDIS, though he usually favours one particular unit. To a Time Lord, their technology is simple: if need be, the Doctor could build himself a new one from scratch in almost no time.

High-kinetic sonic waves can open almost all kinds of mechanical or electronic locks.

A reversed mode can also seal locks – useful when trying to keep an alien werewolf at bay.

The screwdriver's range of functions is almost limitless, including the interception of signals, medical diagnostics, repairing organic parts, operating machinery and scanning new threats – like the Weeping Angels.

Primary emitter cluster

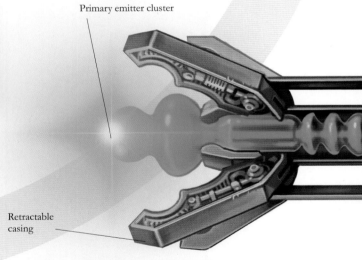

Retractable casing

Sonic screwdrivers are designed to be portable and functional

In the mysterious Library, the Doctor meets River Song. Although she knows him well, for him this is their first meeting. The fact that she has an advanced sonic screwdriver, given to her in the future by the Doctor, is a sign of their strong friendship.

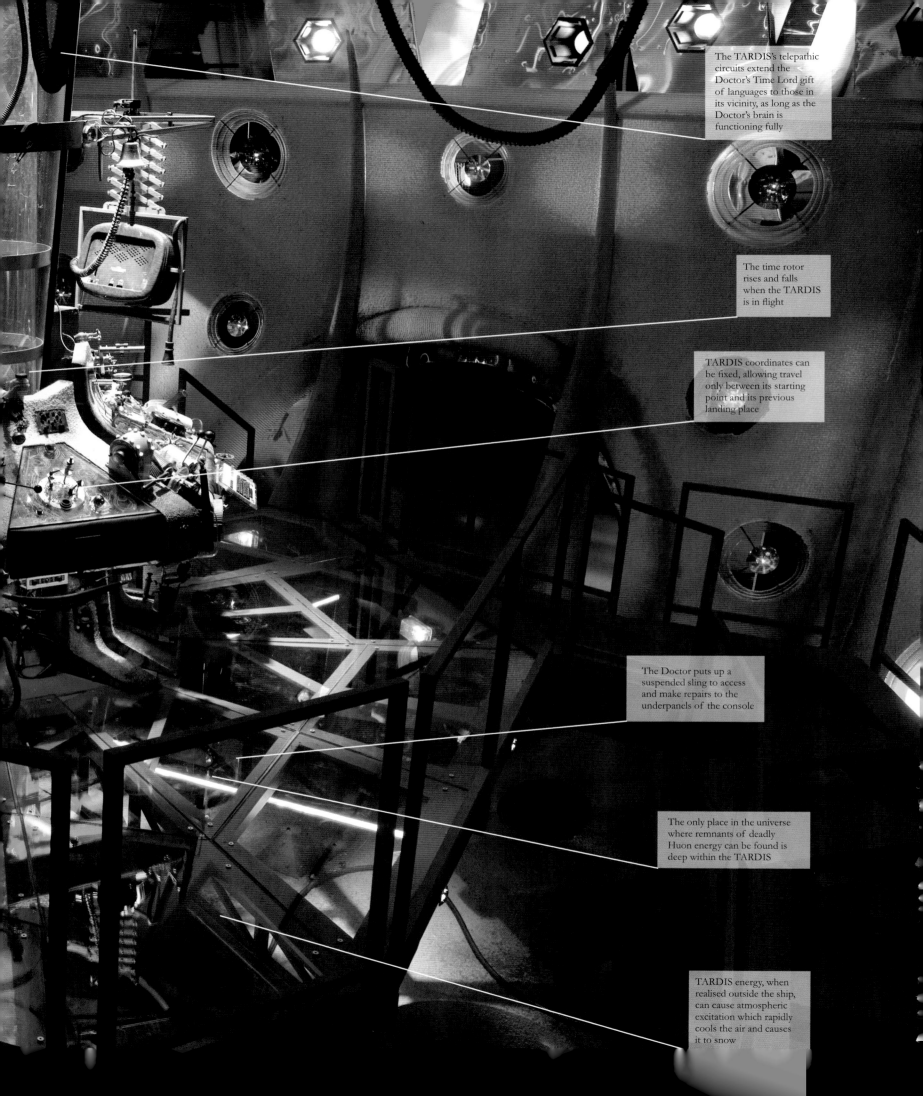

The TARDIS's telepathic circuits extend the Doctor's Time Lord gift of languages to those in its vicinity, as long as the Doctor's brain is functioning fully

The time rotor rises and falls when the TARDIS is in flight

TARDIS coordinates can be fixed, allowing travel only between its starting point and its previous landing place

The Doctor puts up a suspended sling to access and make repairs to the underpanels of the console

The only place in the universe where remnants of deadly Huon energy can be found is deep within the TARDIS

TARDIS energy, when realised outside the ship, can cause atmospheric excitation which rapidly cools the air and causes it to snow

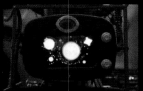

After damage from regeneration energy, the TARDIS reconfigures itself to a different template. The functions – like this atom accelerator – are the same, but they have all-new controls.

This multi-purpose monitor is a window to the outside world. Its live feed shows what's going on beyond the TARDIS as well as displaying statistical data.

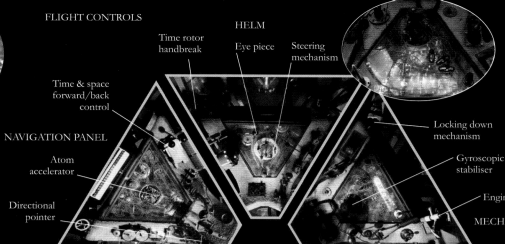

The Doctor has furnished the TARDIS with all kinds of bric-a-brac acquired during his wanderings.

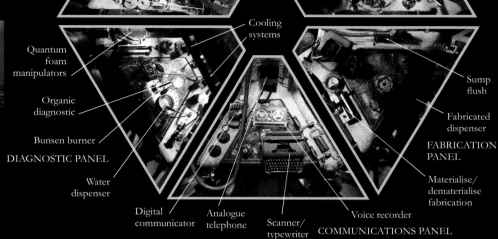

FLIGHT CONTROLS

HELM

Time rotor handbreak

Eye piece

Steering mechanism

Time & space forward/back control

NAVIGATION PANEL

Atom accelerator

Directional pointer

Locking down mechanism

Gyroscopic stabiliser

Engine release lever

MECHANICAL PANEL

Cooling systems

Quantum foam manipulators

Organic diagnostic

Bunsen burner

DIAGNOSTIC PANEL

Water dispenser

Sump flush

Fabricated dispenser

FABRICATION PANEL

Materialise/ dematerialise fabrication

Digital communicator

Analogue telephone

Scanner/ typewriter

Voice recorder

COMMUNICATIONS PANEL

TARDIS Controls
The central console contains all the controls needed to fly the TARDIS. It is here that the Doctor sets the coordinates that determine the time and place of the TARDIS's materialisation.

Walking on Air
An air shell extended from the TARDIS enables Amy to experience the full effect of the cosmos, floating freely and safely in open space.

All Hands on Deck
Although the TARDIS's hexagonal console was designed to have six pilots, the Doctor has been flying solo for years. But after the defeat of Davros and the Reality Bomb, the Doctor is joined by all the old faces, who help as the TARDIS tows Earth back to its rightful position.

Rival Pilot
River Song seems to understand the TARDIS better than the Doctor does. Not only does she fly and land it all by herself, she does so more smoothly than him. She's good, but then she's had a good teacher – a future version of the Doctor.

Cloister Bell
The cloister bell rings if the TARDIS, or the universe itself, is in dire peril. It begins to sound when Rose gives the Doctor her "Bad Wolf" message – code for "the end of the universe" and when the exploding time energy is wiping out the existence of time.

The TARDIS

Materialisation beacon indicates when TARDIS is arriving or departing

THE DOCTOR IS able to travel through time and space using a machine called the TARDIS. A triumph of Time Lord temporal engineering, TARDISes are "dimensionally transcendental" which means that the interior and exterior exist in different dimensions and they can change both their external appearance and internal layout. When the Doctor decided to flee Gallifrey and roam the universe, he stole a TARDIS awaiting servicing for a variety of malfunctions and faults. He has never been able to fully repair it, making his travels often erratic and uncontrolled.

The Doctor's TARDIS is stuck in the shape of a 1960s London Police Box because its chameleon circuit has been damaged

TARDIS exterior is virtually indestructible

TARDIS Facts

- The name TARDIS is an acronym of "Time And Relative Dimension In Space".
- The Doctor's TARDIS is a Type 40TT Capsule, considered obsolete by the Time Lords. There were originally 305 registered Type 40 TARDISes.
- The TARDIS has a "chameleon circuit", which is supposed to change its external appearance to blend in with its surroundings, wherever it lands.
- The TARDIS is able to use its telepathic circuits to translate almost any language for the benefit of its occupants.
- The exterior shell of the TARDIS seems to weigh no more than an ordinary police box: it can be picked up and moved with suitable machinery.

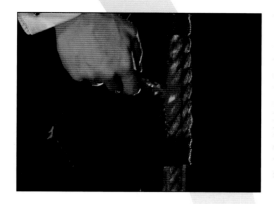

The beam from a sonic screwdriver can interact at a molecular level with another object, for example to "cut" a rope by unravelling the individual fibres at a particular point. It can also produce a high-energy beam capable of generating heat in order to burn or slice through many kinds of material.

Sonic screwdrivers can remotely detonate explosives, such as bombs, and activate missiles. At a certain power setting, it can even blast a door clean off its hinges.

Screwdriver Operation

Sonic screwdrivers contain Gallifreyan circuitry, allowing their operator to switch between different functions using slight adjustments to the exterior casing. However, the device must be directed towards its object for maximum effectiveness. The Doctor keeps the tool on him for as long as its power cells allow between recharges.

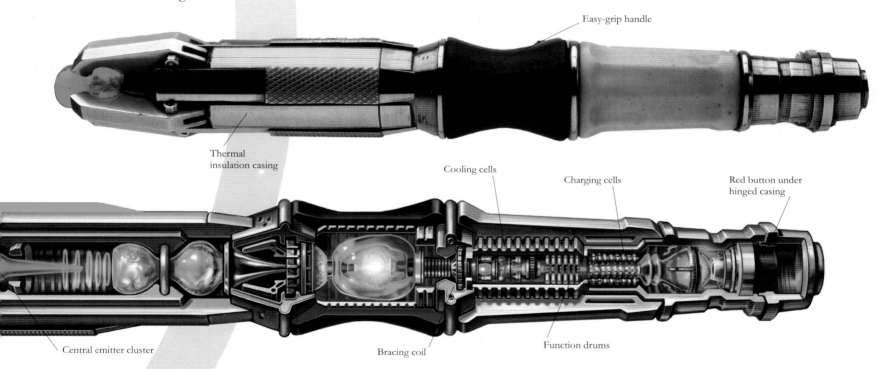

Easy-grip handle

Thermal insulation casing

Cooling cells

Charging cells

Red button under hinged casing

Central emitter cluster

Bracing coil

Function drums

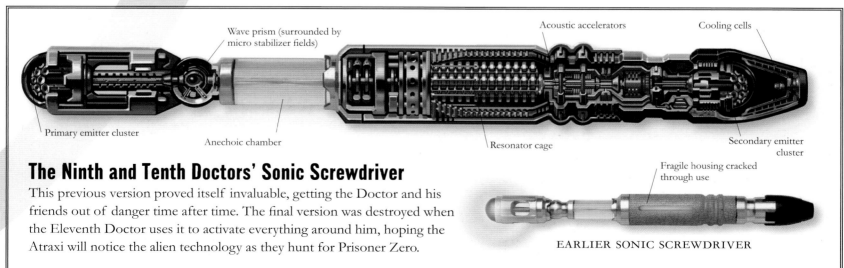

Wave prism (surrounded by micro stabilizer fields)

Acoustic accelerators

Cooling cells

Primary emitter cluster

Anechoic chamber

Resonator cage

Secondary emitter cluster

Fragile housing cracked through use

The Ninth and Tenth Doctors' Sonic Screwdriver

This previous version proved itself invaluable, getting the Doctor and his friends out of danger time after time. The final version was destroyed when the Eleventh Doctor uses it to activate everything around him, hoping the Atraxi will notice the alien technology as they hunt for Prisoner Zero.

EARLIER SONIC SCREWDRIVER

Tools of the Trade

I N ADDITION TO his trusty Sonic Screwdriver, the Doctor has many devices to make life easier for him and his friends. His capacious pockets often produce a piece of technology that is just the thing for defeating a monster, but the Doctor also uses his high-tech knowledge to improvise weapons or handy gadgets. These are just a few of the things he has made use of in his travels.

Page is blank until psychically activated to present an image

Psychic Paper

Psychic paper appears blank but projects a low-level telepathic field, causing the viewer to see whatever they expect to see – such as an invitation or security pass – although it may also reflect what the holder is thinking. The Face of Boe and River Song contact the Doctor for help via his paper, and he has used it to gain entry to many places, such as Adipose Industries and Ood Operations. However, its use is limited: geniuses and individuals with psychic training are not fooled by the paper's trickery.

When the Atraxi threaten Earth, the Doctor uses the paper to gain access to a conference of Earth's scientific experts.

Antiplastic

Antiplastic is a chemical liquid that breaks down plastic into its component molecules on contact. This makes it a useful weapon against creatures made of living plastic such as the Nestene Consciousness.

Possession of the liquid is considered a declaration of war by the Nestene

Parabolic temporal wave shield protects scanner from outside interference

Lammersteen Scanner

Unable to use Time Lord technology in case he discloses his presence to whatever is living above Craig Owens's flat, the Doctor builds this bizarre contraption, based upon the non-technological engineering of Lammersteen, to scan the time interference that is preventing the TARDIS from materialising. He discovers that the flat upstairs is not a flat but a stranded space ship.

Vortex energy spikes send an alarm if the scanner is detected

Lateral balance stabiliser ensures structure will not collapse

Luminosity discharges unused energy as light

External scanner antenna is a back-up alarm

Continuous motion energy matrix maintains power

Handle can be used to lift two tons

Activation switch makes clamp stick to surface

Visual Recognition Device

Knowing your enemy is half the battle and when a person or creature is placed before this gadget's mirror, it displays the name of their species and their planet of origin. The Doctor uses it to find out more about the mysterious Krafayis. The creature is picked up on the machine's screen, even though it is normally invisible to the human eye.

Recognition screen

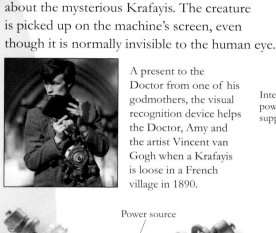

A present to the Doctor from one of his godmothers, the visual recognition device helps the Doctor, Amy and the artist Vincent van Gogh when a Krafayis is loose in a French village in 1890.

Internal power supply

Discovered on Earth by Torchwood operatives

Magna-Clamp

Alien magna-clamps cancel the mass of any object to which they are attached, rendering it virtually weightless. They form an unbreakable bond with any surface, which the Doctor and Rose find useful when they want to avoid being pulled into the Void, while every Dalek and Cyberman is sucked in.

Like much Time Lord technology, the complex machine looks simple

Power source

Gravity Globe

Gravity and light are easily supplied by these portable gravity globes. The Doctor uses one to explore the Aplan Mortarium. By removing the gravity, he, River and Amy are saved from the unanchored Weeping Angels, who fall into the abyss.

Straps for carrying or wearing the device

The Doctor improvises this pathogenesis detector from an ordinary electricity plug, some light bulbs and basic TARDIS technology. It tracks creatures and flashes red whenever alien life forms, such as Adipose, are nearby.

Directional zig-zag plotter couplings provide space/time data

PATHOGENESIS DETECTOR

ELECTROMAGNETIC POWER SOURCE

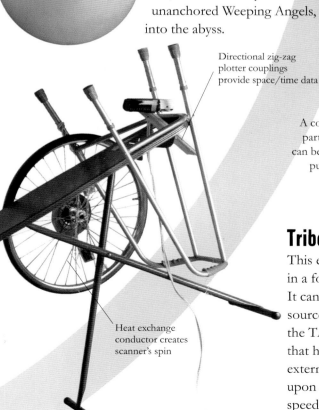

A core component of cyborgs (part-robotic, part-biological creatures), this power source can be used to create a strong electromagnetic pulse that will scramble the circuits of any robot in the vicinity.

Heat exchange conductor creates scanner's spin

Power-level display

Coral from the organic body of the TARDIS

Tribophysical Waveform Macro-kinetic Extrapolator

This extrapolator acts as a pan-dimensional surfboard, shielding its user in a force field and then riding energy waves to a preset destination. It can be programmed to lock onto an alien energy source and take its power. Integrated into the TARDIS, it emits a force field that helps the ship resist external forces exerted upon it and it also speeds up the TARDIS refuelling process.

Amy Pond

Amy knows her own mind, and isn't easily swayed by others

Amy has a great sense of style

Amy loves experimenting with clothes from the TARDIS wardrobe

AMY POND'S LIFE changed when she was seven years old, the day she met the Doctor. Because of a TARDIS malfunction, she had to wait 12 years before she saw him again. Brave, bold and decisive, Amy is a good travelling companion for the Doctor. She is not afraid of dangerous situations, speaking her mind or even challenging the Doctor.

Amy and Her Boys

Amy has had the Doctor on a pedestal since she was a child, but has pragmatically settled with Rory. When the Doctor returns and she travels in the TARDIS, it turns her head and she starts doubting her relationship with Rory. However, adventures eventually reveal the Doctor's infallibility and Rory's strength. With Rory as her boyfriend and the Doctor as, the Doctor, they are happy to tag along as Amy's boys.

Come along, Pond!

Confident and fearless, Amy is ready to deal with anything that comes her way. But a small part of her is still the vulnerable child who was abandoned, first by her parents and then by the Doctor. When he finally turns up again, she is all grown up, but it takes her a while to forgive him.

Perceptive Pond

Amy's insight brings new perspectives to the Doctor. On Starship UK, she sees something in him that he himself can't, and that helps her understand the Star Whale. Like him, it is the last of its race and cannot bear to see children suffer. Recognising this, Amy realises the Star Whale is a willing helper, which saves its life.

Amy Facts

• Amelia Jessica Pond meets the Doctor when she is seven and 19 years old. She is 21 when she meets the Doctor for the third time on the night before her wedding and agrees to travel with him.
• Amelia changes her name to Amy after the Doctor says it sounds like something out of a fairy tale.
• She moved to Leadworth from Inverness when she was very young but has never lost her Scottish accent.
• Amy's parents are Tabetha and Augustus, but she is raised by her Aunt Sharon. When the Doctor resets the universe, time is rewritten meaning that Amy's parents never went away.

Unfazed

Amy is not daunted by famous or powerful people. She doesn't hesitate to take charge of formidable prime minister Winston Churchill when the Daleks threaten Earth. He is impressed with her bravery and leadership, and wishes he had more like her in his war effort against the Nazis.

Brave

Amy is very afraid when she thinks her arm has turned to stone, locking her to a hand rail so she cannot run from the Weeping Angels. Despite her fear, she accepts her fate and is adamant that the Doctor should leave her. She will not hold anyone back. But he knows the stone is only an illusion. He bites her hand, she screams and lets go, and they run together.

Personable

Artist Vincent van Gogh is an unusual character. An outcast in his village, people find him very difficult. Amy isn't intimidated and uses her charms to diffuse a tense situation and win him over. He loves her frankness and passion for life.

THE RAGGEDY DOCTOR

Amy made puppets of the Doctor and put on shows

Papier-mâché models

AMELIA'S DRAWINGS

Amelia carves smiley faces on apples like her mother used to

SMILEY APPLE

When the Doctor returns, he convinces Amy he has only been gone for a few minutes because the carved apple she gave him is still fresh.

Like her grown-up self, Amelia is ready for anything

The crashed TARDIS in Amy's garden

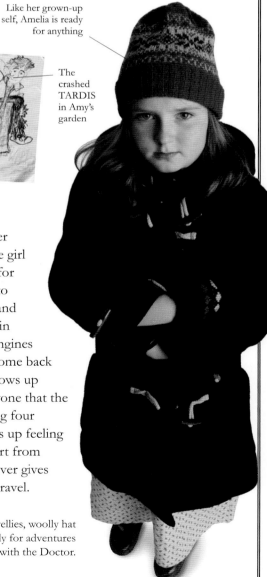

Amelia Pond

Little Amy, called by her full name Amelia, is the girl who waits a long time for the Doctor. He needs to stabilize the TARDIS and promises he'll be back in five minutes. But the engines phase and he doesn't come back for 12 years. Amelia grows up unable to convince anyone that the Doctor is real, including four psychiatrists. She grows up feeling abandoned and set apart from anyone else, but she never gives up her dream of time travel.

Amelia puts on her wellies, woolly hat and duffel coat ready for adventures with the Doctor.

Very little scares Amelia, not even a man in a box falling from the sky in the middle of the night.

Eager to join the Doctor in the TARDIS, Amelia packs her suitcase for travelling the stars.

Rory Williams

RORY WILLIAMS is a straightforward guy, content with his life in sleepy Leadworth so long as he is with Amy Pond, his girlfriend with whom he's besotted. They have known each other since childhood, but he has always felt second-best to Amy's Doctor. Amy even made Rory dress up as him. Rory is astounded to discover that the Doctor is real, and he is worried: a flesh-and-blood rival is a more serious threat than an imaginary friend.

Smart Rory learns about cutting-edge science after meeting the Doctor

Could have been a doctor if he'd applied himself more

The Doctor makes fun of his pointy nose

Rory is always a bit scruffy

A Date in Venice

Life with the Doctor is dazzling and it can blind people to the things that are important. The Doctor has seen it devour relationships and life plans and he senses that Amy has drifted too far from Rory. So the Doctor brings Rory along for a trip in the TARDIS so he and Amy can reconnect. Rory is surprised how distant Amy seems when he'd only seen her a few hours earlier. For her, she's not even sure how long it's been since she saw him.

The Failed Doctor

Compassionate Rory makes a good nurse, but he would have preferred to have been a doctor. He isn't very forceful and struggles to stand up to people who intimidate him, like hospital consultants or even sure-footed Amy. But when it really matters, Rory proves that he is brave and has the strength to stand up to anything to protect those he loves.

Nurse's hosptial scrubs

Amy feels torn between the exciting Doctor and ordinary Rory. However, events in a dream sequence help her realise that Rory is the one for her. In the dream, he is killed by alien Eknodines and she kills herself by crashing a campervan because she'd rather die than live without him.

Having overcome her doubts about Rory, Amy happily marries him. But far from settling down, they leave their wedding party to return to the TARDIS with the Doctor.

Rory and the Doctor

Rory and the Doctor do not hit it off when they first meet. However, when Rory travels in the TARDIS, he witnesses first hand the appeal of the Doctor. The Doctor shows him things he could never have imagined before, and gives him renewed faith in the universe.

Confronted with a Silurian, Rory acts differently from other humans. He feels no fear, but is fascinated by this creature who is his predecessor on Earth. He wants to understand and, even in the face of Alaya's taunts and threats of violence, he displays his humanity by tenderly stroking her face.

Rory works in the Casualty department

The Doctor calls him "Rory Pond" because he's under Amy's thumb

RORY'S HOSPITAL PASS

Rory's work pass gives him and Amy access to Leadworth Hospital when they are tracking Prisoner Zero to prevent the Atraxi destroying Earth.

Rory Facts

- Rory works in the medical profession because of Amy's obsession with the Doctor.
- Amy made Rory dress up as the Doctor when they were children.
- Rory may appear bumbling, but he is insightful: when everyone was filming the Atraxi, Rory was focused on the man with a dog who was supposed to be in a coma.
- Brave Rory takes a bullet for the Doctor when he is shot by a Silurian.
- Rory would give up life on board the TARDIS in a second if Amy wanted to settle down with him. In the mean time, wherever she goes, he will loyally follow.

A New Rory

When Rory is consumed by energy from the cracks in the universe, he ceases to exist. However, in 102 AD, he appears as a Roman centurion. He looks like Rory and believes he is Rory, but he is in fact an Auton: a Nestene duplicate retrieved from Amy's memories. He doesn't age and can live indefinitely, but he is not immortal. His plastic body cannot heal so he must keep away from heat and radio signals.

Skin looks human but has slight plastic sheen

Nestene Possession

Amy and Rory have only just rekindled their relationship when Rory succumbs to Nestene control. He is desperate to be human, but he cannot stop himself from shooting Amy. In order to keep her alive, the Doctor encloses Amy in the stasis-locked Pandorica until he can revive her.

The Boy Who Waited

Rory displays his dedication to Amy by guarding her in the Pandorica Box for 2,000 years. He becomes part of the Pandorica legend as the mystery figure the Lone Centurion. He is written about by Emperor Hadrian, and Isaac Newton and Samuel Pepys call him a friend. The story of the Lone Centurion ends with him carrying the Box from a burning warehouse during the Blitz. However, Rory's story continues: he is by the Pandorica to be reunited with Amy when she is revived in 2010, and is ready to use his Auton weapon to protect her and the Doctor.

Leadworth

THE QUAINT ENGLISH village of Leadworth in rural Gloucestershire is home to Amy Pond and Rory Williams. With little more than a church, a pub, a post office, a fire station and a duck pond, the village is not vibrant, but it does have a strong sense of neighbourliness. Leadworth is the last place you would expect anything out of the ordinary to happen.

Amy's House

Strange disturbances around a space/time crack bring the TARDIS to this house, where Amelia Pond lives with her aunt. The Doctor discovers that Amelia is no ordinary girl: her house has too many rooms and the crack in her wall has been pouring the power of the universe through her dreams.

Life in the village might seem idyllic but it is actually the focus of a terrifying alien threat. A dangerous alien called Prisoner Zero has escaped imprisonment by the Atraxi and is hiding in Leadworth and causing local people to fall into comas. In an attempt to recapture it, the Atraxi threaten to incinerate Earth.

Memorial to those from the Leadworth area who died in the two World Wars

To Leadworth Hospital

Amy doesn't remember ever seeing any ducks on the duck pond

Pub is the heart of village life and the venue for Rory's stag do that is interrupted by the Doctor

Leadworth Hospital

Royal Leadworth Hospital on the outskirts of town is where Rory works as a nurse. The hospital is also the focus of the alien Prisoner Zero when it is on the run from the Atraxi. The multi-form creates psychic links with coma patients and takes on their appearances to disguise itself as human.

Leadworth Church is where Amy and Rory finally say "I do"

To Amy's house

Ruins are all that remain of Leadworth House

Jeff Angelo's house is the site of the Doctor's action to save the world from the Atraxi

Upper Leadworth

The Dream Lord, an incarnation of the Doctor's dark psyche, creates a false reality in Upper Leadworth, a place that time forgot. Five years in the future, Rory and Amy have settled down. Rory has everything he ever wanted: Amy, a home, a baby on the way and a career as a respected doctor. However, Amy feels trapped after the excitement of travelling with the Doctor and is glad to see him return, even if it does spell danger.

Eknodines

The Dream Lord's version of Leadworth has been invaded by Eknodines, who are aliens fleeing their home world. On Earth, they take over the bodies of elderly human hosts. Angered at having been driven from their home, they want to destroy other races. The Eknodines reveal green eye-stalks from the pensioners' mouths. Their tentacles spray a green cloud of lethal gas that can reduce people to dust in seconds.

River Song

ARCHAEOLOGIST-FOR-HIRE River Song is a formidable woman. Exceptionally brave and fiercely loyal, she is a good ally to have, although the Doctor finds her reckless at times. The Doctor and River have always met at different points in their time streams, which makes for a complicated relationship. The Doctor is wary of her because of this but he accepts that their lives are inextricably linked.

Uneasy Alliance

Time travelling ensures that the bond between River Song and the Doctor is complicated. They are always meeting in the wrong order because her past is his future. The Doctor is frustrated that she knows so much about him when he knows so little about her. When he first meets her, he asks her about their relationship, but she refuses to reveal any "spoilers".

Gun's serial number

RIVER'S PISTOL

Fires energy bolts

Made from light-weight material

Getting in Touch

River has such faith that the Doctor will always come to her aid, she's prepared to stake her life on it. When she needs his help to find a Weeping Angel she carves a message for him onto a Home Box aboard a starliner, records her coordinates on it and then jumps out of the ship into space, confident that the TARDIS will appear.

River is imprisoned in a Stormcage containment facility for murder. The incident is shrouded in mystery but her victim was a good man and a hero to many and – according to Song – the best man she's ever known. Could she be referring to the Doctor?

Is River the Doctor's wife?

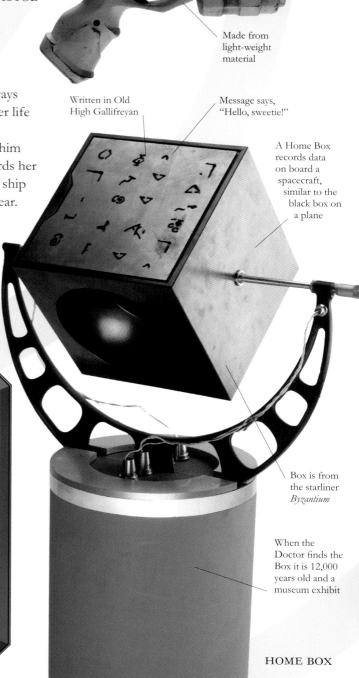

Written in Old High Gallifreyan

Message says, "Hello, sweetie!"

A Home Box records data on board a spacecraft, similar to the black box on a plane

Box is from the starliner *Byzantium*

When the Doctor finds the Box it is 12,000 years old and a museum exhibit

HOME BOX

River Song Facts

- River is thought to be the only person who knows the Doctor's real name.
- Although she has neither confirmed nor denied it, River is possibly the Doctor's wife in the future.
- River has intimate knowledge of Time Lords: she can write in Old High Gallifreyan, the lost language of the Time Lords, and is aware that if both of his hearts are damaged, the Doctor might not regenerate.
- To allow her to recognise the Doctor, her diary contains pictures of all his different faces.
- River has her own sonic screwdriver, given to her by a Doctor of the future.

Hello, Sweetie

Confident and used to getting her own way, River treats the Doctor with a familiarity that no one else would presume to have. She enjoys showing off and revells in the fact that she can fly the TARDIS better than he can. He isn't used to finding himself on the back foot, but they still make a good team.

Extraordinary Explorer

River Song is no ordinary archaeologist. An expert in her field and highly experienced, she has led many treacherous expeditions. She is well trained in the use of military weapons and has a full array of gadgets like hallucinogenic lipstick and callisto pulses disguised as earrings. Her meeting in the Library with the Doctor is his first, but her last. She courageously sacrifices herself to save everyone in the Library but especially to keep the Doctor alive, because she knows how important he is to the future.

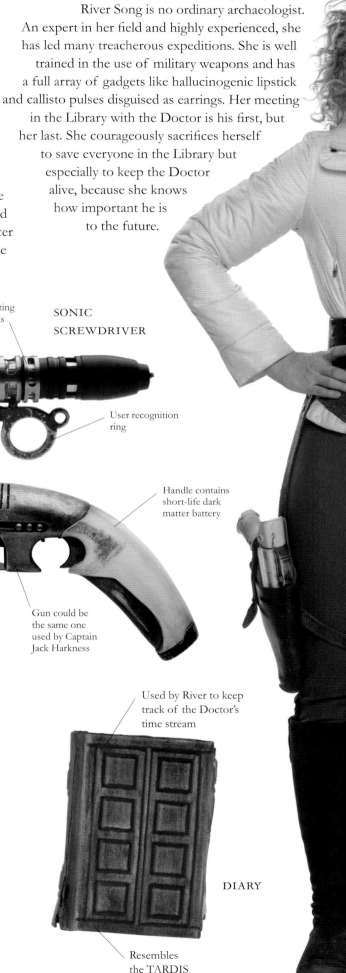

RIVER SONG

SONIC SCREWDRIVER

Enhanced emitter lense is superior to the current Doctor's screwdriver

Wave amplifiers

Master function key houses neural relay

Setting dials

User recognition ring

TARDIS remote return

Can switch between different functions: Sonic Cannon, Blaster and Disruptor

Handle contains short-life dark matter battery

Fires sonic waves which form pulsing squares of blue light that can cut through thick walls and also has a reverse function

SQUARENESS GUN

Gun could be the same one used by Captain Jack Harkness

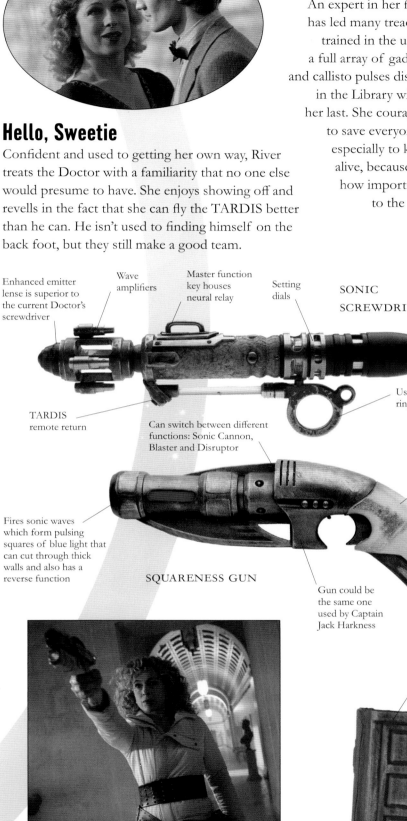

In the National Museum, River is confronted with a stone Dalek. It expects her – as one of the Doctor's companions – to show mercy. It's a fatal mistake. Unsentimental River has no qualms about shooting dead a Dalek.

Used by River to keep track of the Doctor's time stream

DIARY

Resembles the TARDIS

Captain Jack Harkness

Jack has never revealed his true name

B ORN IN THE BOESHANE PENINSULA, "Jack" was recruited to the Time Agency, a mysterious espionage organisation, but left after it stole two years of his memory. Used to the free and easy ways of the 51st century, and blessed with natural good looks and winning ways, he put his enormous charm to work as a conman, taking the identity of a Captain Jack Harkness.

Stranded on Earth in 1869 after leaving Satellite 5, Jack moves to the site of Cardiff's Rift to wait for the Doctor. He is recruited by Torchwood Three. In 2000, he becomes leader and builds a team including Ianto Jones and Gwen Cooper.

A Change of Heart

After meeting the Doctor, Captain Jack discovers unexpected levels of courage and selflessness and leaves his criminal ways. They become good friends and before the Tenth Doctor's regeneration, he finds Jack to say goodbye and introduces him to Alonso Frame, a member of the *Titanic* crew, in the hope that they will be happy together.

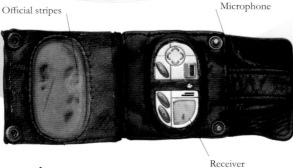

Official stripes

Microphone

Receiver

JACK'S VORTEX MANIPULATOR

Immortality

When Rose opens the heart of the TARDIS and absorbs the Time Vortex, she gains its tremendous powers. With her abilities, she raises Jack from the dead after he is exterminated by the Daleks on Satellite 5. But she cannot control these all-consuming powers, and Jack is returned, not for one lifetime, but forever.

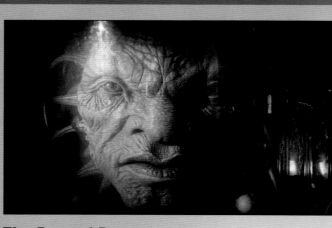

The Face of Boe

What happens to an immortal who keeps ageing? Jack had been a poster boy in the Boeshane Peninsula, earning the nickname "the Face of Boe". The Doctor has met another Face of Boe – an ancient giant alien head. Is this who Captain Jack will become after billions of years?

The Face of Boe sacrifices himself to free the people of New Earth, and imparts his dying secret to the Doctor: "You Are Not Alone". This hint that the Master is living as Professor Yana at the end of the universe gives a clue to the fact that the Face of Boe has been to the far future as Captain Jack.

Donna Noble

Fiery red hair matches her fiery temper

Confident face in public hides self-doubt

S HE WAS A LOUDMOUTH who hated Christmas, could not point to Germany on a map and deep down thought she was worthless. But being with the Doctor allows Donna to see herself in a new way. She shows she has compassion and sense, and when she saves the cosmos from Davros's Reality Bomb, Donna is the most important woman in the whole universe.

Donna missed the Sycorax invasion (hungover) and the Cybermen (scuba-diving in Spain), but she has front row seats for the Racnoss.

Unlikely Friends

Donna and the Doctor do not exactly hit it off when they first meet, but they go on to form a strong friendship. Knowing his death is near, the Tenth Doctor returns to check on her. She has found love but is struggling financially. Making use of a perk of time travel, he gives her a winning lottery ticket as a wedding present.

Life Without Donna

Being with Donna changes the Doctor and it turns out that without her there would be no Doctor at all. A beetle belonging to a being known as the Trickster reveals an alternate timeline in which Donna never met the Doctor and he was killed by the Racnoss.

TRICKSTER'S BEETLE

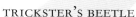

Attaches itself to victim's back

Can only be seen by those with psychic abilities

Donna's compassion influences the Doctor. When they visit Pompeii she convinces him to save Caecilius's family and she shares responsibility for destroying the city so he doesn't have to bear the weight alone.

Smart suit for office work

Wilfred Mott

A keen amateur astronomer with an interest in aliens, Wilf adores his only grandchild. Unlike Sylvia, he thinks that Donna should go with the Doctor as it is a once-in-a-lifetime opportunity to explore the stars. And it turns out not just to be Donna who is important to humanity – Wilf has his own role to play in saving the world from the Time Lords and the Doctor sacrifices his tenth incarnation to save him.

Sylvia Noble

Sylvia cannot forgive the Doctor for helping to ruin Donna's wedding and does not want her daughter to go away with him. Deep down she is proud of Donna, but she is not very good at showing it.

The Doctor-Donna

When the Daleks capture the TARDIS, only Donna and the Doctor's severed hand are on board. Somehow they fuse, creating a human Doctor and giving Donna the knowledge of a Time Lord. The all-new Doctor-Donna is the only thing that can save the universe from Davros. But a Time Lord brain is so powerful that a human host cannot survive. The Doctor must say goodbye: if she ever remembers him, she will die. He cannot attend her wedding, but he watches from a safe distance.

Cannot believe how much running is involved in being with the Doctor

Rose Tyler

LONDON TEENAGER Rose Tyler's world is transformed the night she is attacked by possessed mannequins. A mysterious stranger called the Doctor saves her life and offers her a way out of her dull life as a shop assistant – a chance to travel across the universe. But this amazing adventure comes at a cost. Rose must leave behind her mum, who is also her best friend, her boyfriend, Mickey, and the life she knows on Earth.

When she looks into the heart of the TARDIS, Rose absorbs the energy of the time vortex. It gives her great power over time and space, but starts to destroy her. The Doctor sacrifices his ninth incarnation to save her.

Stranded

Rose is thrilled by her exciting life with the Doctor, whom she begins to realise she loves. But her time with him comes to a sudden end when she is sucked into a parallel world. She comes back to this reality in times of great need, but must always return.

A New Life

At first, Rose is overawed by life with the Doctor, but she soon takes to time travel with gusto. She is quick witted, intelligent and determined – assets that make her the ideal travelling companion. Best of all, Rose has a wicked sense of humour that makes their adventures together fun.

Her job at Henrik's department store meant Rose got a discount on clothes

A Companion for Rose

Rose's foray into this reality helps foil Davros, but she must still return to her parallel life. Despite their love, the Doctor cannot join her. However, his human version – created from his hand and a human – can. He is just like the Doctor, except that he is Rose's own kind.

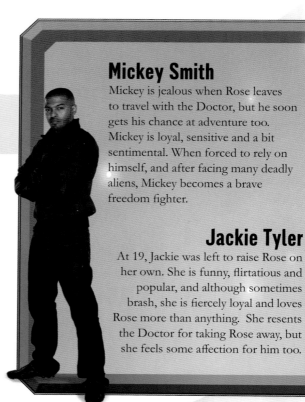

Mickey Smith

Mickey is jealous when Rose leaves to travel with the Doctor, but he soon gets his chance at adventure too. Mickey is loyal, sensitive and a bit sentimental. When forced to rely on himself, and after facing many deadly aliens, Mickey becomes a brave freedom fighter.

Jackie Tyler

At 19, Jackie was left to raise Rose on her own. She is funny, flirtatious and popular, and although sometimes brash, she is fiercely loyal and loves Rose more than anything. She resents the Doctor for taking Rose away, but she feels some affection for him too.

Wears white
medical coat
with pride

UNIT call sign is
Greyhound Six

Smart,
fashionable
appearance
befits a
professional
woman

Martha Jones

CAPABLE AND INDEPENDENT, 23-year-old medical student Martha Jones impresses the Doctor right from the beginning. When the Royal Hope Hospital is transported to the moon by the rhino-headed Judoon, Martha remains calm while all around her panic. Within hours of meeting the Doctor, she not only saves his life, but manages to save Earth too.

Medical student

From the start, Martha is less in awe of the Doctor than his previous companion Rose was. As a medical student, she is comfortable in the world of science and has a quick understanding of the complex concepts his world revolves around. She spends much of her time feeling second best to Rose, but her actions show that she is just what the Doctor ordered.

Martha is compassionate and positive. When the war-mongering Sontarans create a clone of her for their army, it looks into her mind, with all her hopes and dreams, and changes allegiance as it dies.

Spreading the Word

When the Master ravages life on Earth, Martha becomes a legend by spreading hope and telling stories of the Doctor around the world. But her success wipes out her celebrity: the hero is forgotten when the Master is defeated and time is reversed.

Family Ties

Martha learns that families and the Doctor do not mix when her family are used as pawns by the Master. She feels responsible for their suffering and gives up time-travelling to keep them safe from future danger.

A United Front

With Martha's record of saving the world, it is no surprise that the Unified Intelligence Agency (UNIT) – the organisation tasked with defending Earth – want Martha on their medical staff. It might look like she has become a soldier, but principled Martha is working from the inside to stop the fighting. The Doctor taught her well.

Torchwood

Torchwood Facts

- Security firm HC Clements acted as one of London Torchwood's many fronts for 23 years.
- Torchwood Three was charged by Queen Victoria with policing the Rift in Cardiff.
- There is a Torchwood Four, but no one, not even Captain Jack, knows its location.
- Torchwood is a top-secret organisation – very few are supposed to know of its existence. Drugs are used to erase the memories of those who find out about it.

I N 1879, QUEEN VICTORIA VISITED Torchwood House in Scotland, where she met the Doctor, and discovered the existence of aliens. Determined that the British Empire would be ready for its next extraterrestrial visitors, she founded the Torchwood Institute to protect Britain and its territories from aliens – with the Doctor listed as enemy number one. Bases were established in London (Torchwood One), Glasgow (Torchwood Two) and Cardiff (Torchwood Three).

Over the years, the Torchwood Institute moved from defending against aliens to exploiting their technology, its motto being: "If it is alien, it is ours." Under Yvonne Hartman, this attitude led to a battle between Daleks and Cybermen at Canary Wharf and the destruction of the Torchwood Institute.

Torchwood Tower was built to reach a spatial breach 600 feet above sea level.

Captain Jack has worked at Torchwood for over a century

Torchwood Three's HQ, the "Hub", is found under the Oval Basin in Cardiff's Bute Docks

Window was originally a marine outlet pump

Hub may be entered via an invisible lift in Roald Dahl Plass, or a disused Tourist Information Centre

Powerful and mysterious Rift Manipulator

The Hub has many levels, reaching deep underground

A New Torchwood

After the exploitative and aggressive Torchwood regime was destroyed in the Battle of Canary Wharf, Captain Jack re-established Torchwood with a new ethos. Based in Cardiff, it returned to its original principle of defending the Earth.

Jack in Charge

Captain Jack recruited a new team to run Torchwood Three: Suzie Costello, Dr Owen Harper, Toshiko Sato and Ianto Jones. Costello was later replaced by police officer Gwen Cooper. Jack is fiercely loyal to his team, even to the point of turning down an opportunity to rejoin the Doctor to stay with them. He inspires loyalty in return, although his refusal to explain his past can cause resentment.

The Doctor puts aside his animosity towards Torchwood and asks for its help after the Earth is abducted by Daleks. Ianto and Gwen use the Rift to provide the power needed to tow the planet back home.

UNIT

T HE UNIFIED INTELLIGENCE TASKFORCE
(UNIT) was set up in the late twentieth century
to deal with the alien menaces facing humankind. Although its
remit is similar to Torchwood's, UNIT is a predominantly military
organisation. The Doctor spent several years as UNIT's scientific
advisor after he was exiled to Earth by the Time Lords for
meddling in the affairs of other planets.

The Valiant

UNIT's flagship is an aircraft carrier with a difference – it
floats in the air, not on the sea! It was designed by evil Time
Lord the Master while he was masquerading as Mr Saxon and
working for the Ministry of Defence, and he later made it his
base of operations on Earth. After the Master's defeat, UNIT
readopted the ship – but not before checking it thoroughly
for any Time Lord tricks. Colonel Mace uses its strong
engines to disperse the Sontarans' poisonous gas.

UNIT is based in Geneva but has
branches worldwide. The British section
(HQ: London) was headed for many
years by the Doctor's friend Brigadier
Lethbridge-Stewart. Colonel Mace
is currently in charge. The US forces
(HQ: New York) are commanded by
General Sanchez.

UNIT Weaponry

After years of fighting alien menaces, UNIT has amassed
a stock of unusual weapons, each with a very specific
purpose. Silver bullets are kept in case of a werewolf
attack, while anti-Dalek shells are troops' best hope of
defeating Daleks. Gold-tipped bullets are reserved
for Cybermen, and following recent intelligence,
rad-steel coated bullets have been added to the
arsenal to overcome Sontaran defences.

UNIT
"wings"
cap badge,
adopted in
the 1990s

Teleport operates when
both cords are pulled

Technology salvaged
from the Sontarans

OSTERHAGEN KEY

Three
Osterhagen
stations must
be online to
use the Key

When Earth faces destruction
from Davros, Martha is sent
by UNIT to prepare the Key
for detonation

Twenty-five nuclear warheads have been placed at strategic
locations under the Earth's crust, so that if the suffering of the
human race reaches crisis point, they can be detonated by the
holder of the Osterhagen Key.

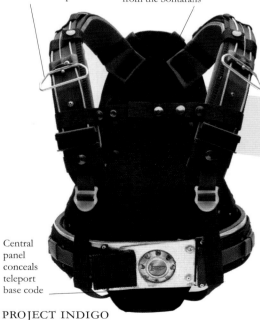

Central
panel
conceals
teleport
base code

PROJECT INDIGO

UNIT's experimental teleport, Project Indigo, is
untested, has not got coordinates and is not stabilised
– it is a possible death trap. But Martha uses it anyway
because she is UNIT's only hope of finding the Doctor
when Davros threatens the whole universe.

UNIT Facts

- Martha Jones gets a job as a UNIT medical officer following
the Doctor's recommendation.
- The Doctor is still officially a member of UNIT, never
having resigned. However, he has never considered himself
bound by the organisation's rules and regulations.
- UNIT and Torchwood reluctantly share intelligence
and resources, and staff are occasionally seconded
between organisations.

Troops
are always
battle-ready

Despite their
remit, many UNIT
soldiers never
encounter aliens

Sarah Jane Smith

FEARLESS REPORTER Sarah Jane Smith travelled with the Third and Fourth Doctors, but when he was suddenly recalled to Gallifrey he left her behind on Earth, without even saying goodbye. When the Doctor didn't return, Sarah Jane assumed he was dead. Many years later, they are reunited and they continue to meet when danger threatens. He turns up to stop her wedding, which is a ploy created by a Trickster to make her forget her life defending Earth.

Thirty years after he left without saying goodbye, the Doctor meets Sarah Jane when they happen to be investigating strange events at a school, though she doesn't recognise his tenth incarnation.

Sarah Jane Facts

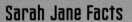

- Sarah Jane's adventures with the Doctor led her to pursue a career investigating occurrences that were too strange or dangerous for other journalists to explore.
- When the Doctor builds a third version of his robot dog, K-9, and sends it to Sarah Jane with his fondest regards, she realises he hadn't forgotten her after all.
- Since settling back into life on Earth, Sarah Jane has never married or had any children.

Mr Smith

After travelling with the Doctor, Sarah Jane is aided in her adventures by supercomputer Mr Smith. He was created through a union between her laptop and a Xylok crystal, which scans for alien threats from its attic hideaway. Mr Smith can also link up with all the telephone exchanges in the world.

Saving the Universe

When Davros and the Daleks transport Earth to the Medusa Cascade to destroy the universe, Sarah Jane is held captive on Davros's Command Ship along with a group of the Doctor's other companions. Captain Jack adapts a warp star of hers to destroy the ship, though it isn't necessary when Donna Noble, enhanced with Time Lord knowledge, defeats Davros.

After Davros's plan is thwarted, Sarah Jane helps to pilot the TARDIS and tow Earth back to its position in the solar system.

Motherhood

An alien race called Bane created a boy from DNA samples in a quest to find the archetypal human. The boy is rescued by Sarah Jane, who names him "Luke" and adopts him as her son.

K-9

LOYAL AND FEARLESS, boasting vast memory banks and highly sophisticated sensors, K-9 became indispensable to the Doctor during his fourth incarnation. He travelled everywhere with the Doctor and would defend him at all costs. When the Doctor's companion, Leela, decided to remain on Gallifrey, K-9 stayed with her. The Doctor then built a replacement, K-9 Mk II, and a third model was sent to Sarah Jane Smith. After K-9 Mk III is blown up defeating the Krillitane, the Doctor presents Sarah Jane with K-9 Mk IV.

Thirty years after the Doctor gave him to Sarah Jane, K-9 is in a bad way. The British climate and salted roads have taken their toll, but fortunately the Doctor is on hand to repair his old friend.

Old Friend

A brilliant doctor named Professor Marius created the first K-9 in the year 5000. Posted to a medical station near Titan, Marius needed a mobile computer and laboratory to assist him. Put together from available parts, Marius styled K-9 after his beloved pet dog on Earth.

K-9 Facts

• After the first K-9 helped the Doctor defeat a sentient virus, the robot's maker, Professor Marius, gave his creation to the Time Lord so he could assist him on his travels.

• According to the Doctor, K-9's design is the height of fashion in the year 5000.

Tracking sensors

DATA-COM PROBE (EXTENDED)

Sensor can analyse all known substances

Multi wavelength optical spectrum sensor

Gravitronic brain enables K-9's artificial intelligence

Data-com probe (retracted)

Signal booster antenna

Operator's manual console

Photon blaster

Name tag contains tracking beacon

Each K-9 model has been equipped with a photon blaster in the snout. Like many human colonists, Professor Marius was wary of potential space threats.

Storage for fully buffered deutronic battery

Removable cover to primary drives

All-terrain protective alignment buffer

John Smith

JOHN SMITH – THE MOST ordinary of names – has often been the Doctor's alias of choice when wanting to blend in. But, when the Tenth Doctor needs somewhere to hide from the deadly Family of Blood, he not only adopts the name, but actually becomes John Smith. The Family are able to track a Time Lord anywhere in time or space, so the TARDIS rewrites the Doctor's DNA so he truly is human.

The Doctor's real life seeps through into John Smith's dreams, which he records as fiction in what he calls his "journal of impossible things". The TARDIS, Rose and many monsters feature, as well as memories of the Earth's future such as the Great War (1914–1918).

From Doctor to Teacher

The Doctor has visited history but John Smith merely gets to teach it. The TARDIS places him in Herefordshire in 1913 as a history teacher at Farringham School for Boys. The disguise is so complete that Smith believes he has always been human and is the Nottingham-born son of watchmaker Sydney and nurse Verity. He is an ordinary man of narrow experiences who knows nothing of the Doctor.

FOB WATCH

Time Lord can communicate from within

Perception filter makes it seem like an ordinary watch

Decorated with Gallifreyan symbols

Mortar board is symbol of authority

Human body take the appearance of the tenth Doctor

A product of his time, Smith approves of corporal punishment

Human senses are dull in comparison to a Time Lord's

Teacher disguise built on Doctor's love of knowledge

Smith relies on books for historical information

The Chameleon Arch

The TARDIS's chameleon arch can alter a Time Lord's physiology to any compatible species without affecting his outer appearance. Once transformation is complete, a Gallifreyan fob watch – a symbol of the Time Lords' mastery over time – stores the original memories, personality and biological data, which are restored the moment the watch is opened.

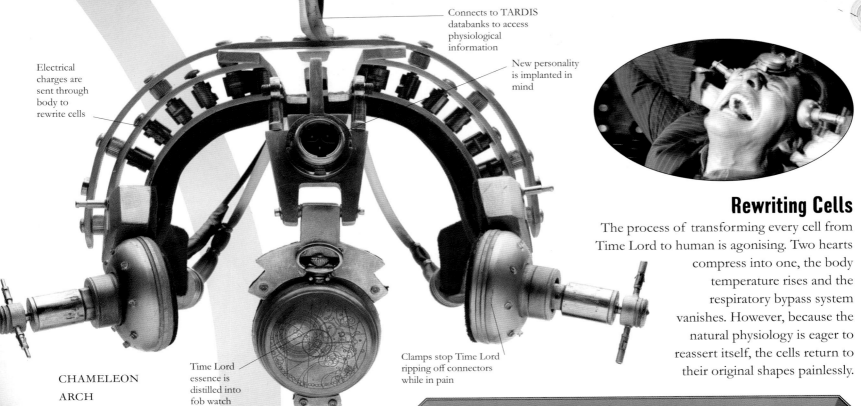

Electrical charges are sent through body to rewrite cells

Connects to TARDIS databanks to access physiological information

New personality is implanted in mind

CHAMELEON ARCH

Time Lord essence is distilled into fob watch

Clamps stop Time Lord ripping off connectors while in pain

Rewriting Cells

The process of transforming every cell from Time Lord to human is agonising. Two hearts compress into one, the body temperature rises and the respiratory bypass system vanishes. However, because the natural physiology is eager to reassert itself, the cells return to their original shapes painlessly.

The Doctor in Love

Nurse Joan Redfern, a young war widow, is the Matron of Farringham School. Joan's unassuming but caring personality appeals to shy and insecure Smith. As an ordinary man, he can see the beauty in an ordinary woman. It is only natural that when two people are thrown together, a bond may develop – but falling in love is something the Doctor never allowed for in his plan.

Martha is the only one who knows the truth about John Smith. The Doctor has trusted her with his life, but in the meantime she has to endure the racism, sexism and classism of the early 1910s – even from John Smith himself.

John Smith's Decision

When the Family's sense of smell tracks down the Doctor, Martha reveals his true identity to John Smith. But opening the fob watch is not straight-forward – it would mean the end of John Smith.

John Smith must choose which to follow: the life of a human, who loves and ages, or the eternal, lonely life of a Time Lord. Time energy from the fob watch lets him see what could happen if he stays human. In 1915, he marries his true love, Joan Redfern.

The next year, 1916, John experiences the overwhelming joy of holding his baby for the first time. He and Joan will have two daughters and a son.

Fifty years later, after a long and happy life, filled with love from his wife, children and grandchildren, John breathes his last breath. The Doctor – virtually immortal – will never experience mortality like this.

John Smith cannot bear to give up his life, but he realises he must sacrifice his chance of happiness for the greater good. Once back as the Doctor, however, he cannot imagine exchanging a Time Lord existence for a human one again!

Daleks

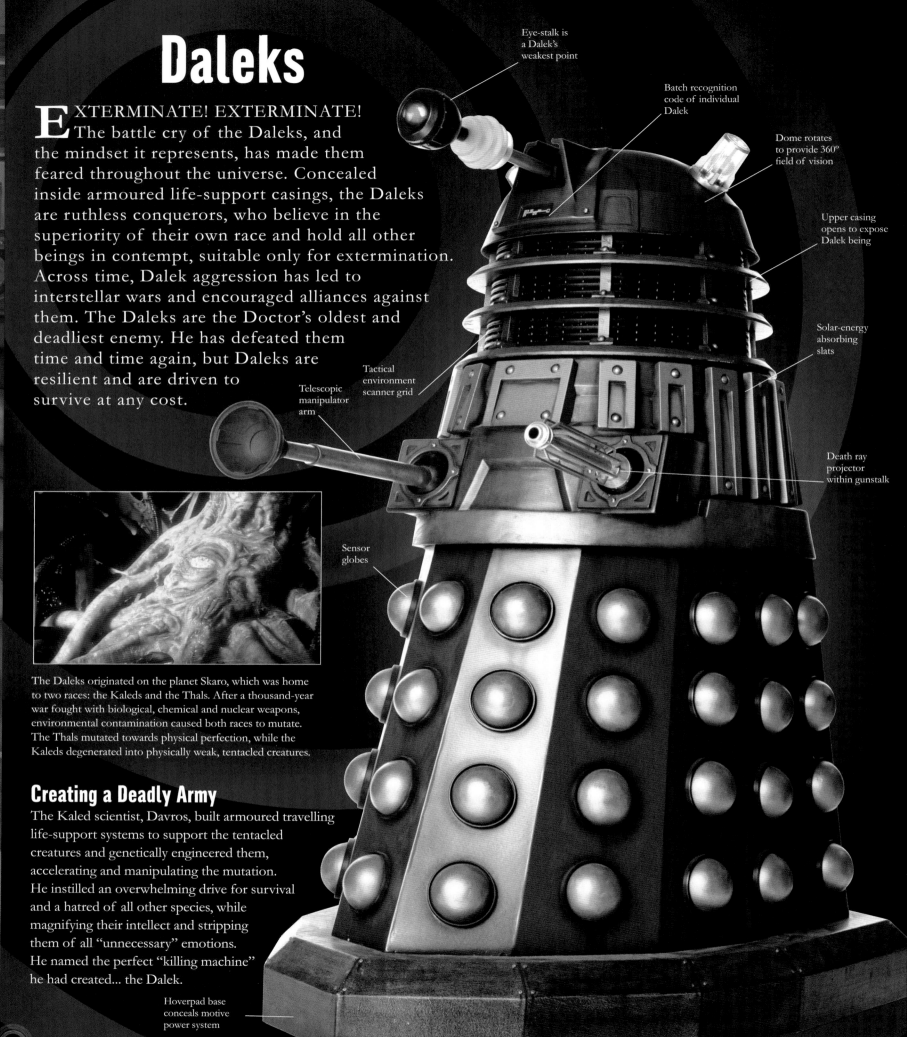

EXTERMINATE! EXTERMINATE! The battle cry of the Daleks, and the mindset it represents, has made them feared throughout the universe. Concealed inside armoured life-support casings, the Daleks are ruthless conquerors, who believe in the superiority of their own race and hold all other beings in contempt, suitable only for extermination. Across time, Dalek aggression has led to interstellar wars and encouraged alliances against them. The Daleks are the Doctor's oldest and deadliest enemy. He has defeated them time and time again, but Daleks are resilient and are driven to survive at any cost.

Eye-stalk is a Dalek's weakest point

Batch recognition code of individual Dalek

Dome rotates to provide 360° field of vision

Upper casing opens to expose Dalek being

Solar-energy absorbing slats

Tactical environment scanner grid

Telescopic manipulator arm

Death ray projector within gunstalk

Sensor globes

The Daleks originated on the planet Skaro, which was home to two races: the Kaleds and the Thals. After a thousand-year war fought with biological, chemical and nuclear weapons, environmental contamination caused both races to mutate. The Thals mutated towards physical perfection, while the Kaleds degenerated into physically weak, tentacled creatures.

Creating a Deadly Army

The Kaled scientist, Davros, built armoured travelling life-support systems to support the tentacled creatures and genetically engineered them, accelerating and manipulating the mutation. He instilled an overwhelming drive for survival and a hatred of all other species, while magnifying their intellect and stripping them of all "unnecessary" emotions. He named the perfect "killing machine" he had created... the Dalek.

Hoverpad base conceals motive power system

Extermination Tools

Each warrior Dalek is equipped with a ray gun and a manipulator arm. The "death ray" is a directed energy weapon that can stun or kill. The manipulator arm can interface with computer systems or mimic hand movements with its "sucker" made of morphic material.

The brilliant and psychotic Davros created the Daleks.

A Dalek's death ray gun uses a ray beam to destroy every cell in a human body.

A Dalek's arm is strong enough to crush a human skull, but it can also kill by extracting all brain waves.

"Sucker" can create powerful vacuum

Arm extends to twice its length

MANIPULATOR ARM

DEATH RAY GUN (FRONT VIEW)

Nitrid barrel

Amplifier tubes manipulate strength of beam to stun or kill

Acceleration chamber projects energy beam

DEATH RAY GUN (SIDE VIEW)

Beam initiation generator

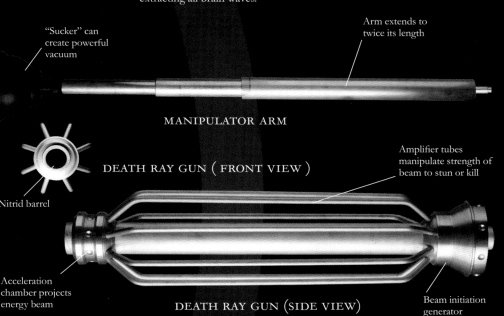

Dalek Point of View

The eye-stalk of the Dalek battle armour provides enhanced vision in the natural colours of Dalek sight. Inbuilt multi-spectral sensors also allow the Dalek to see in infra-red, x-ray and ultra-violet modes. The single eye-stalk is a Dalek's weakest point as it has no back-up system.

On the Warpath

The Daleks have waged war across time and space since their creation, but the complexities of time travel, and the Time Lords' attempts to change Dalek history, make a comprehensive timeline of their battles and invasions difficult. Here are some of their attempts at conquest:

• Generations after their initial creation, Daleks on Skaro were still battling the Thals, when they were first encountered by the Doctor in his first incarnation.

• While chasing the first Doctor through time, a Dalek execution squad fought, and was defeated by, the robot Mechanoids in the 23rd century. This was the beginning of a long war between the two races.

• The Daleks fought another long war, over many centuries, with the android Movellans from star system 4-X-Alpha-4, as both tried to expand their stellar empires. When that war became stalemated, the Daleks travelled through time to seek help from their ancient creator, Davros.

• Reviving Davros led to the development of factions within the Dalek hierarchy and a series of civil wars between different groups supporting and opposing Davros.

• In the 22nd century the Daleks twice invaded Earth, the first time after the destruction of World War III and later, around Earth year 2164, intending to turn it into a giant battleship to aid their wars of conquest.

• By the year 4000 the Daleks planned a master strike to conquer the galaxy with the aid of similarly power-hungry allies. When the Doctor defeated their plans, the alliance self-destructed and embroiled the Daleks in new conflicts.

• Learning of the Time Lords' attempts to thwart their creation, the Daleks attacked Gallifrey and the last Great Time War began.

• Although Gallifrey was destroyed in the attempt to wipe out the Daleks, the Cult of Skaro and the Emperor survived. By the year 200,100, the Dalek Emperor had rebuilt the Dalek race, but it was then destroyed by Rose Tyler.

The Dalek's casing is made from Dalekanium, an extremely robust bonded polycarbide material. It can be penetrated by bastic-tipped bullets, so the Daleks created an energy shield for additional protection.

Dalek battle armour is designed to open up, so that repairs, system enhancements and medical treatments can be carried out. Even without its weaponry, the Dalek is a dangerous creature and has been known to kill.

To avoid capture or to atone for failing a mission, a Dalek is fitted with a self-destruct system for complete obliteration. The components of this system are mounted in the Dalek's sensor globes, which are capable of free flight.

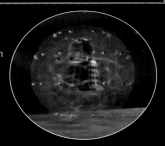

Equipped with anti-gravity generators and gyroscopic stabilisation systems, Daleks can glide across any terrain or hover over any obstacle – even a steep staircase is no hindrance.

Dalek Flagship

EMERGING FROM HIDING above Earth, the Dalek fleet is armed, dangerous and all-powerfully gigantic. The massive Flagship that commands the fleet transports the Dalek Emperor, who is worshipped as a god by the rest of the Daleks. The Emperor is wired into the ship's systems, operating them by his mind, and from them to the rest of the fleet – allowing him total control.

Hidden Army

When it became clear that the Daleks were about to be wiped out in the Great Time War, a single ship managed to slip away into 'the dark spaces'. The badly hurt but functioning Dalek onboard spent centuries in hiding. Slowly, it hatched a secret plan to harvest humans from Earth to supply the genetic material needed to rebuild an army of Daleks under his Imperial command.

Flagship Facts

• The Flagship was used during the Great Time War between Daleks and Time Lords.
• The Dalek Emperor intends to create "Heaven on Earth" by bombing the planet until its landmasses are reduced to radioactive rubble.

• Rose utterly destroys the Dalek fleet when she gains god-like powers from looking into the time-space vortex at the heart of the TARDIS.

Hull strengthening plate

Entire ship armour-plated in spaceship-grade dalekanium (bonded polycarbide metal)

Hull damage from the Great Time War

Signal transmitter ring

Heavy polycarbide rivets

Ship energy-shielding pulses

Rotating dome and outer ring create spin that propels ship

Giant hangar openings located around the central disk allow millions of Daleks to emerge at once into the void of space, heading towards Earth.

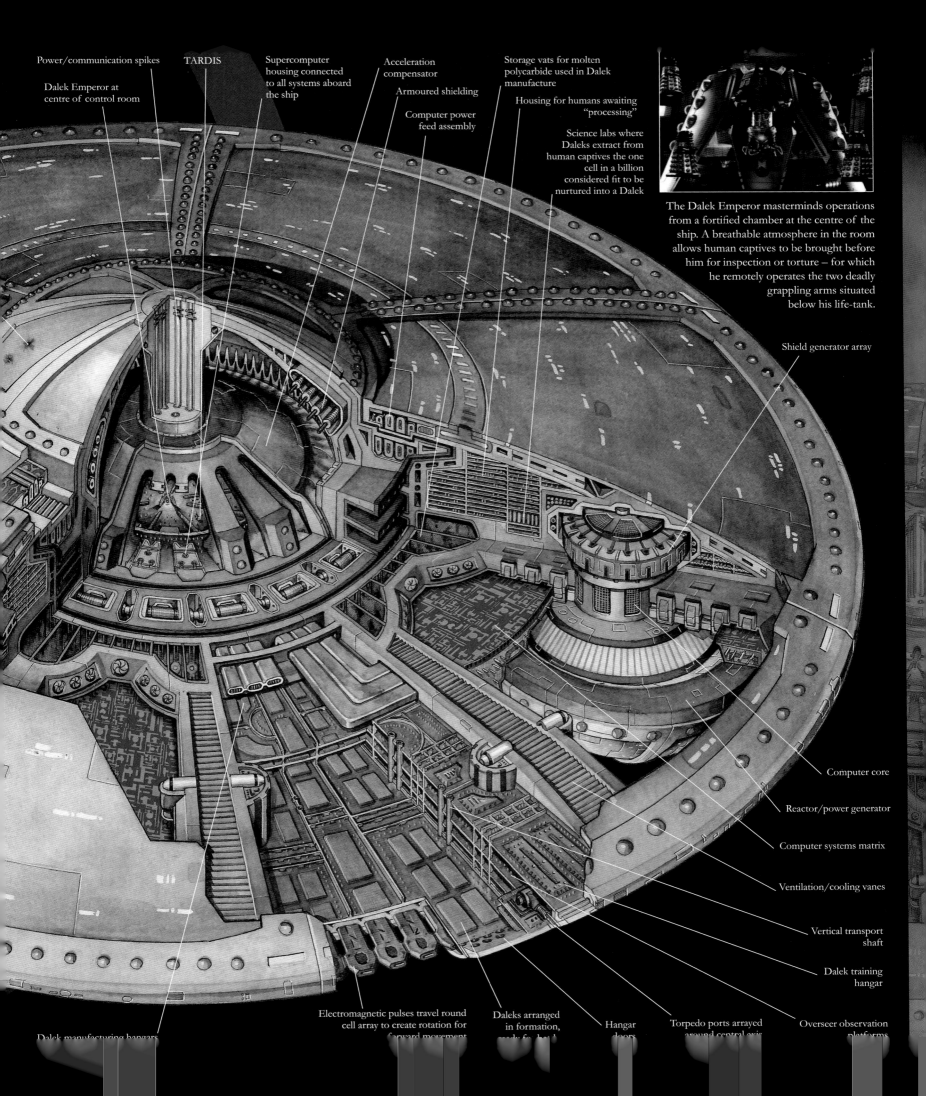

Power/communication spikes

TARDIS

Dalek Emperor at centre of control room

Supercomputer housing connected to all systems aboard the ship

Acceleration compensator

Armoured shielding

Computer power feed assembly

Storage vats for molten polycarbide used in Dalek manufacture

Housing for humans awaiting "processing"

Science labs where Daleks extract from human captives the one cell in a billion considered fit to be nurtured into a Dalek

The Dalek Emperor masterminds operations from a fortified chamber at the centre of the ship. A breathable atmosphere in the room allows human captives to be brought before him for inspection or torture – for which he remotely operates the two deadly grappling arms situated below his life-tank.

Shield generator array

Computer core

Reactor/power generator

Computer systems matrix

Ventilation/cooling vanes

Vertical transport shaft

Dalek training hangar

Dalek manufacturing hangars

Electromagnetic pulses travel round cell array to create rotation for forward movement

Daleks arranged in formation, ready for battle

Hangar doors

Torpedo ports arrayed around central axis

Overseer observation platforms

Torchwood

The Torchwood Institute's mission is to acquire and analyse alien hardware and use it for the good of the British Empire. Torchwood One has its headquarters in Canary Wharf, in the Docklands area of London.

Lever activates shift programme

Torchwood originally discovered a dimensional breach when it appeared as a radar black spot, 180 metres above the ground. The breach was opened when particle engines were fired at the spot.

The Void Ship

This hypothetical craft was designed to exist outside space and time, travelling between dimensions. The sphere fills all who go near it with foreboding. In theory it does not exist because it lacks both radiation and atomic mass.

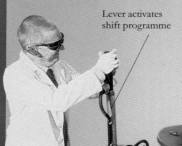

When the Void Ship activates, lab screens go wild. Suddenly, the object has height, mass and an electromagnetic field. The Sphere Chamber doors immediately seal shut to put the area in automatic quarantine.

Inside the Sphere

A sinister casket is concealed inside the Void Ship. Known as the Genesis Ark, it has dimensionally transcendental Time Lord technology similar to the TARDIS, and was used during the Great Time War for the sole purpose of imprisoning the armies of the Time Lords' deadliest enemy – the Daleks.

The Genesis Ark

WHEN THE SECRETIVE Torchwood Institute Two attempts to harness energy from a spatial disturbance over London, it unwittingly breaks through a wall between dimensions. A sinister metal sphere emerges through the breach, which the Doctor instantly recognises as a Void Ship. Sensing that nothing good can be inside it, the Doctor urges Torchwood to send it back through the Rift.

FRONT VIEW

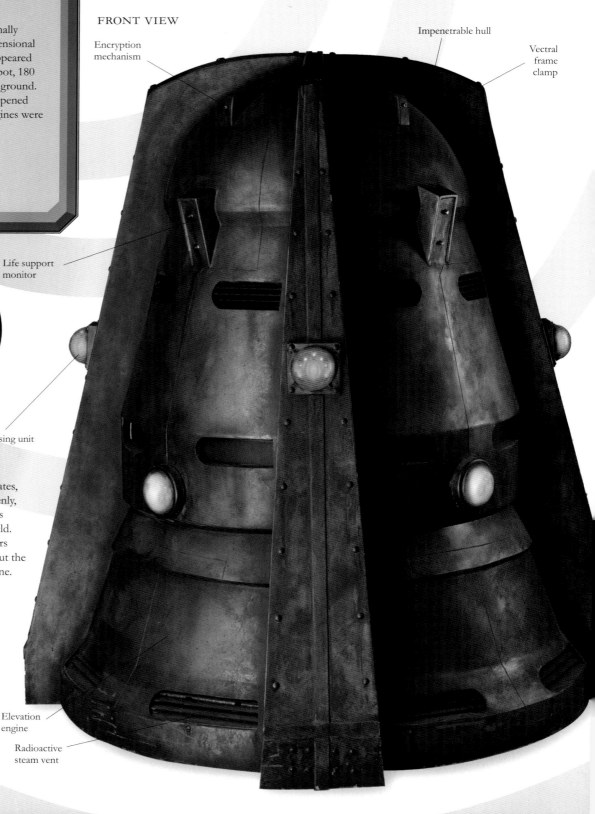

Encryption mechanism

Impenetrable hull

Vectral frame clamp

Life support monitor

Sensor processing unit

Elevation engine

Radioactive steam vent

The Key to the Ark

Rose and Mickey witness the Genesis Ark and four Daleks – the Cult of Skaro – emerging from the Void Ship. The Daleks must keep Rose and Mickey alive because a time-traveller's touch is the key that opens the Ark. As humanoid time-travellers, Rose and Mickey soak up the universe's background radiation – the power source for the Ark. When fighting rages between Daleks and Cybermen in the sphere chamber, Mickey is shoved against the Ark and touches it, causing it to activate.

The lab doctor, Dr Singh, volunteers information to the Daleks, but, in a sickening display of brutality, each Dalek attaches its sucker to his head and extracts his brain waves. Dr Singh collapses on the floor, a withered husk.

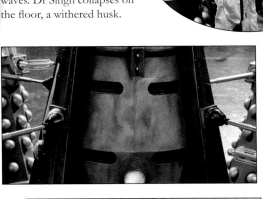

Internal power drive activated

Handprint radiation primes mechanisms

Life support system powers up

Priming console activated

The Cult of Skaro Daleks circle the Ark at intervals and begin the awakening process by attaching their suckers to the four priming consoles on each side of the casket. Rose asks the Black Dalek, Sec, what is inside. It replies, "The future!"

The Ark's Purpose

As the Ark is activated in the sky above London, the Doctor finally understands what the Daleks meant by "Time Lord science". Like the TARDIS, the Ark is much larger on the inside than on the outside. It was used as a prison ship for the millions of the Daleks captured during the Great Time War.

The Black Dalek overrides the roof mechanism of the Torchwood hangar area, elevating the Ark the 48 square kilometres needed for activation.

High over London, the Doctor and his companions watch in horror as the Ark disgorges its evil cargo – millions of Daleks come shooting out in all directions, intent on extermination.

Doomsday Ghosts

Comms device is connected to brain tissue

WHEN THE VOID SHIP bursts through the breach in time and space, it is followed by a small army of humanoid, ghostly figures. Torchwood learns how to open and close the breach and allow the ghosts into their dimension. Every day at midday, Torchwood runs a "ghost shift". For a few minutes it opens the breach a fraction and more ghosts enter. The Doctor warns that the sphere must be sent back and the ghost shifts stopped.

Cyberghosts

People welcome the humanoid ghostly entities, believing them to be departed loved ones. When the breach is finally forced open to 100 per cent, the true nature of the "ghosts" is revealed – as millions of Cybermen materialise, and the steel soldiers commence their invasion.

Although the Torchwood CEO cancels the ghost shifts after the Doctor's warning, some staff ignore her orders and continue opening the breach. The Doctor sees that they are being controlled via cyber ear-pieces. Using his sonic screwdriver, he disrupts the signal and the staff collapse on their desks, dead.

CYBER EAR-PIECE

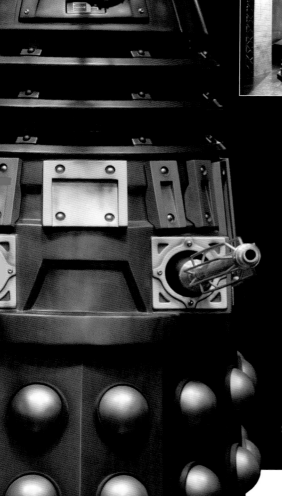

Rival Races

As soon as the Void Ship opens, Daleks and Cybermen detect each other's presence. Both sides send envoys to investigate and the Cyber Leader addresses the Daleks on screen, beginning an historic exchange between the rival races.

Dalek and Cybermen Facts

- Daleks do not form alliances unless they can perceive a way of gaining a further advantage, usually achieved by betraying their allies.

- Daleks are confident of beating five million Cybermen, even with a single Dalek. They regard this not as war, but as "pest control".

- Dalek force fields absorb Cybermen laser blasts, rendering them ineffective. Cybermen have no such force field and can be instantly exterminated.

- Daleks measure time in "rels". Ordering the recording of the Cyberleader's message to be rewound 9 rels, they identify a Dalek enemy on the screen, standing behind the Cyber Leader. Rose confirms that they have seen the Doctor.

- Daleks and Cybermen have never encountered each other before. Communication opens with both sides refusing to identify themselves first to the other.

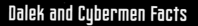

Parallel Worlds

A squad of humans from a parallel Earth materialise into the Torchwood Institute and blast the nearby Cybermen. By infiltrating their parallel Earth's Torchwood, the humans obtained a Parallel World Transporter that allows them to cross between worlds. The Cybermen have escaped from their parallel Earth into this one.

BLASTER

Power cell

Barrel

Aim

Safety catch

Range finder

Gas cartridge chamber

Cooling fins

Pump-action blast mechanism

Energy couplings

Neck strap

Grip-adhesive stock

Transporter disc

Charged metal alloy

Above: By opening the blaster's bonding chamber the Doctor adapts it to be effective against polycarbide – the exterior of a Dalek.

Right: The Parallel World Transporter is worn around the neck and can only transport one person at a time safely.

PARALLEL WORLD TRANSPORTER

The Battle of the Sphere Chamber

In a temporary alliance with the Cybermen, the parallel-world humans storm the Sphere Chamber after the Doctor blows its doors open with his sonic screwdriver. Caught off-guard, the Daleks' casings are impaired by the energy blasts and it is some moments before they can adapt their weaponry. In the chaos of the battle, the Doctor rescues Rose and Mickey.

As the scale of the Dalek threat becomes clear, the Cyberleader declares an emergency and calls all units to converge on Torchwood. Immediately, the Cybermen abandon guard over their human captives and march in formation to meet the Dalek army.

The Battle of Canary Wharf

Dalek legions emerge from the Genesis Ark and begin a spectacular battle with the Cybermen. Dalek Sec orders his airborne forces to exterminate all life forms below, sending terrified people diving for cover. But the Dalek supremacy is short-lived. The Doctor opens the breach once more, sucking almost every Dalek and Cyberman back into the Void.

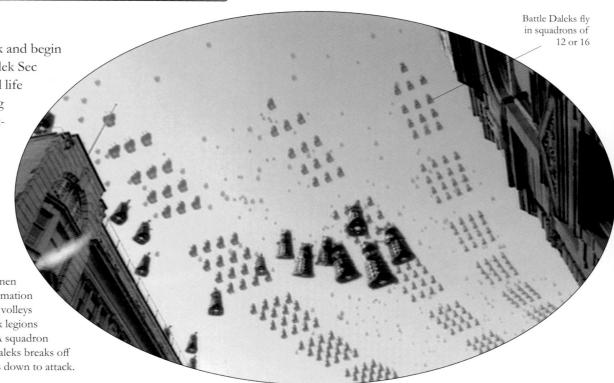

Battle Daleks fly in squadrons of 12 or 16

The Cybermen stand in formation to fire laser volleys at the Dalek legions overhead. A squadron of battle Daleks breaks off and swoops down to attack.

The Cult of Skaro

A SECRET ORDER OF Daleks, the Cult of Skaro, consists of four members. Their role is to think like the enemies of the Daleks in order to find new ways of exterminating them. They exist outside the normal Dalek hierarchy, above even the Emperor. To emphasise their special status, they even have individual names.

Dalek Sec

The utterly ruthless Dalek Sec is the Black Dalek leader of the Cult of Skaro, guiding the research of his colleagues. To escape the failure of the Genesis Ark plan, Sec transports the four members of the Cult away, using an emergency temporal shift.

Swivelling eye-stalk and rotating dome provide almost spherical field of vision

Dalek is equipped with automatic distress call if casing is breached or forced open

Force field broadcast antennae. Each flat panel broadcasts an overlapping field for complete coverage around the Dalek

Rotating mid-section gives Dalek 360° range of fire

Death ray beam is a focused electrical discharge of immense power

Sensor globes capable of free flight to provide remote battlefield intelligence

Luminosity discharge valve dissipates excess energy from Dalek's cells, through light and sound emission

Sensor grid louvres allow waste heat exhaust

Manipulator arm's telescopic tube and swivel mount provide tremendous reach

The Cult members escaped the destruction of the Dalek race at the end of the Great Time War by fleeing in a Void Ship with the captured Genesis Ark. Their ship used a spatial disturbance to break through to Earth.

Dalekanium outer casing is lightweight, yet incredibly strong and able to resist energy weapons

"Sucker" tool, made of morphic material, can assume various useful shapes

Hoverpad base with anti-gravity generators enables Dalek to hover and fly

DALEK SEC

Special Training

The Cult of Skaro members have a strong bond of loyalty to each other, and are fanatically driven by the need to use their special training to extend the Dalek Empire throughout space and time. Under the leadership of the Black Dalek, the Cult dedicates its existence to finding new ways to exterminate the Daleks' adversaries, by creatively thinking in "non-Dalek" ways. Like their leader, each Dalek is assigned its own name and personality, in the belief that understanding and mimicking the individuality of many of their enemies will allow them to discover new and more terrifying ways to overcome them.

Cult of Skaro Facts

• The Cult of Skaro consists of four members, led by Dalek Sec. This small number can be strategically useful, but they are too few to be a military threat to the Emperor.

• The Cult is named after the Dalek homeworld Skaro, which was devastated by a supernova generated by the seventh Doctor's subterfuge with the Hand of Omega. The planet was finally obliterated during the Great Time War.

• In order to "think like the enemy", the Cult Daleks are encouraged to develop their imaginations.

• Unlike ordinary Daleks, Cult members do have limited emotions, which mimic those of other life forms. They also have a sense of self-preservation not found in Dalek warriors.

• The Cult's existence was kept so secret by the Daleks that even the Doctor thought they were a legend.

DALEK CAAN

DALEK JAST

DALEK THAY

The Genesis Ark is actually a captured Time Lord prison ship, containing millions of Daleks.

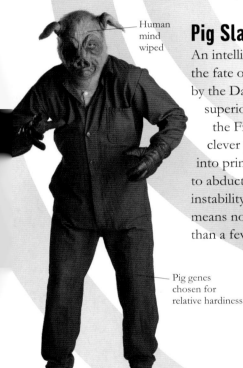

In 1930, New York City is in the grip of an economic depression, with mass unemployment and thousands destitute. The Doctor and Martha turn up here soon after the Daleks arrive by emergency temporal shift.

Dalek Sec

AS LEADER OF THE CULT OF SKARO, Dalek Sec is tasked by the Dalek Emperor with finding new ways for Daleks to breed and prosper. Following a failed plan to grow Dalek embryos, the ambitious Sec comes up with a radical idea: purity has led to near extinction for the Daleks, so he decides their biological destiny lies with humans, in what he calls the Final Experiment.

Pig Slaves

Human mind wiped

An intelligence scan determines the fate of the humans captured by the Daleks. While those of superior intelligence are kept for the Final Experiment, the less clever prisoners are transformed into primitive pig slaves and used to abduct more people. The instability of the genetic graft means no pig-man survives more than a few weeks.

Pig genes chosen for relative hardiness

Energy Converter

Dalek Sec's plan to forge a new Dalek-human race requires a powerful energy source. A huge solar flare is due to pass by Earth, and will provide the necessary Gamma radiation. The Daleks must attract the flare and conduct its energy, so they engineer and build the tallest point in New York — the Empire State Building.

Dalek mutant merges with human brains

Dalekenium casing acts as chrysalis during transformation

Chromatin solution stimulates genetic changes

Dalek Sec is so dedicated that he is willing to experiment upon himself. He becomes the first ever Dalek-human hybrid.

Casing and weapons discarded after metamorphosis

Becoming Human

The other three members of the Cult of Skaro — Daleks Thay, Jast and Caan — believe that Daleks should remain pure, but Sec disagrees. He is convinced that a genetic merger with human beings will herald the beginning of a new era of Dalek rule.

Human brain creates emotions

Tentacles from Dalek mutant

Exposed flesh makes hybrid vulnerable

Hybrid gains dextrous finger

Mr Diagoras's suit is a remnant of a former identity

Dalek-Human Hybrid

Ambition, hatred, aggression and a genius for war – that is what Dalek Sec thinks being human is all about. When he combines with the ruthless and ambitious Mr Diagoras, he believes he is getting more of the same. But Sec discovers something unexpected – positive emotions. He decides that Daleks must return to emotions – both positive and negative ones.

Dalekanium is attached to mast

Empire State Building Facts

• The Empire State Building in New York was opened to the public in 1931.
• The cost of the Art Deco-style building was $24,718,000. It was expected to cost twice as much, but expenses fell due to the Depression.
• Construction took one year and 45 days, and finished ahead of schedule.
• The building has 102 floors and the top of the lightning rod is 443.20 metres above ground.
• It was the tallest building in the world for 40 years, until the World Trade Center was built.

Death in Hooverville

Soloman, the leader of Hooverville, cares for the outcasts of this New York shanty town, but when he tries to extend the hand of friendship to the Daleks, he is exterminated. However, his courage inspires Dalek Sec, who feels compassion for the first time.

The purpose of Daleks is to be supreme! Sec's fellow Daleks disagree that their race should renounce their purpose by embracing emotions and becoming humanised. They declare their one-time leader to be an enemy of the Daleks and he is exterminated while compassionately trying to save the Doctor's life.

Dalek Humans

Human DNA is spliced with Dalek Sec's genetic code, creating a new race. But some Time Lord gets in the mix, and so the humanoid Daleks begin to question orders. This leads to their extermination, but not before they kill Dalek Thay and Dalek Jast.

Dalek Caan

With the Daleks Sec, Thay and Jast all dead, Dalek Caan is the only surviving member of the Cult of Skaro – the last Dalek in the universe. Caan rejects the Doctor's offer of help, operates his emergency temporal shift and vanishes.

Davros

D AVROS IS RESPONSIBLE for the Daleks. The scientist foresaw a day when the chemical warfare that raged on his home planet would cause his people, the Kaleds, to mutate. Obsessed with the survival of his race, he experimented with their mutations and invented an armoured machine to carry them. Ambitious Davros went further, making chromosomal changes to Dalek embryos to remove their consciences and emotions. But his plan backfired when his creations declared him unnecessary to their plans and attempted to kill him.

Davros and the Doctor

The Doctor has a grudging respect for a number of his adversaries, but Davros is not one of them. The Time Lord has come to regard Davros as one of the most dangerous, and certainly the most insane, of his many enemies. The Doctor is appalled, but unsurprised, to discover that Davros's reaction to the horror and devastation of the Time War is a desire to destroy all living things.

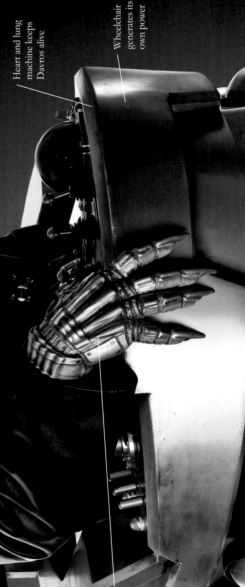

Davros taunts the Doctor, claiming that he is responsible for innocent deaths, despite his abhorrence of violence. Davros asserts that the Doctor takes ordinary people and turns them into weapons to die in his name.

Like many children with their parents, the Daleks' relationship with Davros is a combination of reverence and contempt: they look to him to solve their problems, but still believe that they are better off without him.

Davros Facts

- Calling himself "the Great Healer", Davros once ran a funeral parlour, where he raised money to build a Dalek army by selling cryogenically frozen bodies as human food.
- Davros's planet, Skaro, was destroyed during the Time War.
- Davros offers to reward loyalty in human followers with immortality – by turning them into Daleks.
- The Doctor once asked Davros if he would wipe out all life if he had the opportunity – an idea Davros found fascinating and that came back to haunt the Doctor.

Single lens replaces sightless eyes

Microphone and amplifier enable speech

Voice becomes more Dalek-like when angry

Heart and lung machine keeps Davros alive

Wheelchair generates its own power

Mechanical hand shoots energy bolts

Chair inspired the design of the Dalek shell

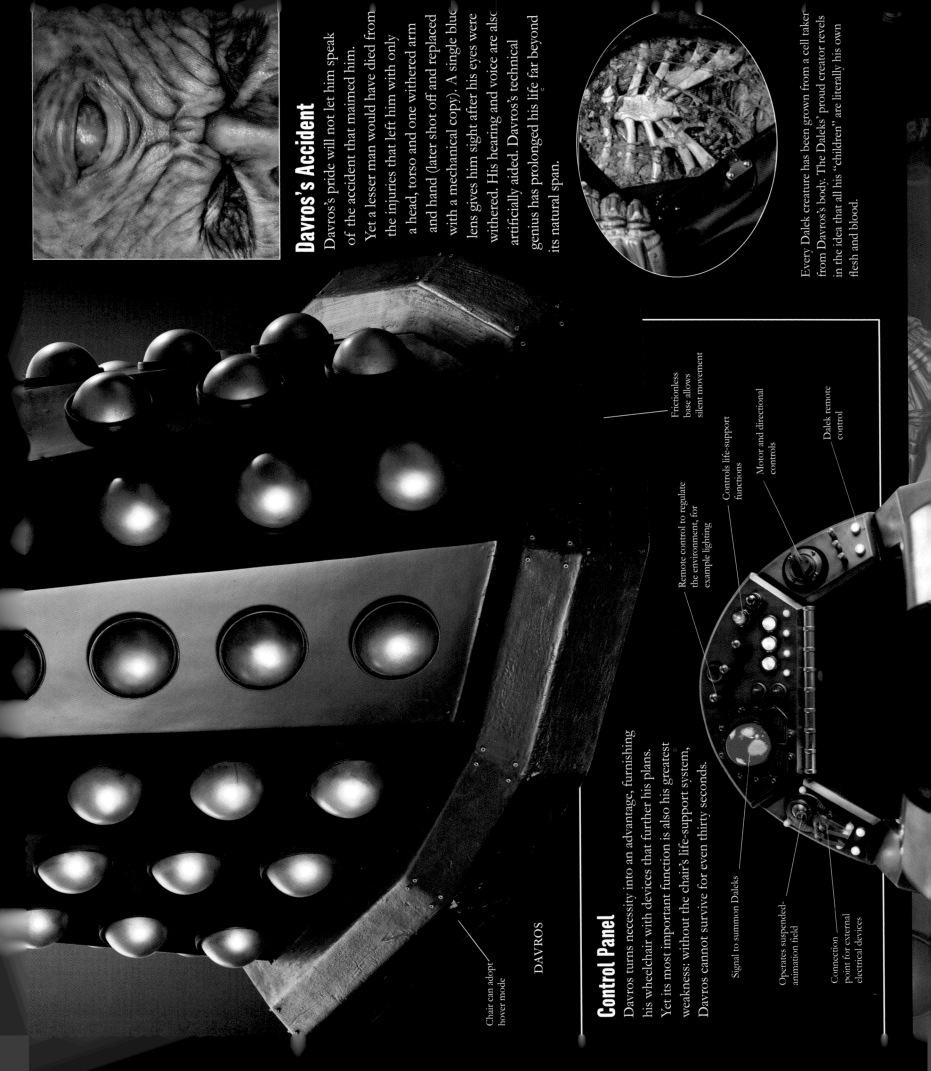

Davros's Accident

Davros's pride will not let him speak of the accident that maimed him. Yet a lesser man would have died from the injuries that left him with only a head, torso and one withered arm and hand (later shot off and replaced with a mechanical copy). A single blue lens gives him sight after his eyes were withered. His hearing and voice are also artificially aided. Davros's technical genius has prolonged his life far beyond its natural span.

Every Dalek creature has been grown from a cell taken from Davros's body. The Daleks' proud creator revels in the idea that all his "children" are literally his own flesh and blood.

Frictionless base allows silent movement

Controls life-support functions

Motor and directional controls

Dalek remote control

Remote control to regulate the environment, for example lighting

Chair can adopt hover mode

DAVROS

Control Panel

Davros turns necessity into an advantage, furnishing his wheelchair with devices that further his plans. Yet its most important function is also his greatest weakness: without the chair's life-support system, Davros cannot survive for even thirty seconds.

Signal to summon Daleks

Operates suspended-animation field

Connection point for external electrical devices

Davros's Empire

MEGALOMANIAC DAVROS has only one ambition — to see a universe ruled by Daleks. His warped mind believes that co-operation between species is impossible and ultimately only one race can survive; he is determined that race will be the Daleks. His plans are based on the Daleks exterminating their way to victory, annihilating every other being in the universe. This apocalyptic short-cut will make Davros Emperor of an empty infinity.

The Reality Bomb

In order to build his empire and destroy all life forms other than the Daleks, Davros creates the Reality Bomb. This fearsome technology cancels out the electrical fields that hold together atoms, obliterating the fabric of reality itself. Davros brings the Doctor to his Command Ship, the Dalek *Crucible*, for a ring-side seat at what he believes will be his ultimate victory.

Lights flash in time with speech

The Supreme Dalek

Although Daleks were engineered to have no emotions, the Supreme Dalek is guilty of pride when he believes that the Daleks have finally triumphed over the Doctor. His strength and determination see him retain control as other Daleks falter, but he meets his end thanks to Captain Jack's Defabricator Gun.

The Supreme Dalek was charged with activating the Reality Bomb

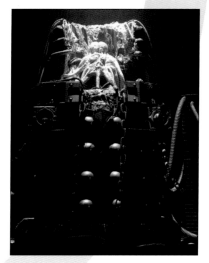

Dalek Caan

The only surviving member of the Cult of Skaro, Dalek Caan went insane when he jumped into the Time War to save Davros. This mind-altering experience brought him the gift of prophecy.

The Dalek Command Ship, the *Crucible*, has a core of deadly z-neutrino energy

The Medusa Cascade

Twenty-seven celestial bodies, including Earth, Adipose 3, Pyrovillia, Callufrax Minor, Jahoo, Shallacatop, Woman Wept, Clom and the Lost Moon of Poosh, vanish from their normal orbits and appear together in the Medusa Cascade. This is not chance, but careful design by crazed Davros. In their new formation, with the Dalek *Crucible* at their centre, they function as a transmitter designed to focus the wavelength of the Reality Bomb.

Masters of Earth

Once again, Daleks terrorize the citizens of Earth. This time, however, the Daleks set their sights higher than the destruction of the human race: Earth has a role to play as part of the machinery of the Reality Bomb.

The Subwave Network

The Subwave Network is a piece of undetectable sentient software used to seek out and communicate with anyone who can help to contact the Doctor. With its power sufficiently boosted by the computer Mr Smith, it is able to transmit to the Doctor, even though he is separated in time.

Ex-Prime Minister Harriet Jones feels responsible for Earth's citizens, and sacrifices her life to help contact the Doctor.

The Secret Army

The Subwave Network enables the Doctor to communicate with Captain Jack Harkness, Sarah Jane Smith and Martha Jones – previous companions of the Doctor, collectively called "the Children of Time" by Davros. The Doctor is horrified when Davros claims the Doctor turns his friends into weapons to fight his battles for him.

Mr Copper's foundation and Harriet Jones created the Subwave Network.

The Shadow Proclamation

Nearly all species recognise the authority of the Shadow Proclamation, an imposing galactic regulatory body and police force that both sets and enforces laws. Its directives proscribe alien interference with planets and their populations, and govern the rules of parlay between species.

Distinctive albino appearance

Headquarters of the Shadow Proclamation

Architect speaks on behalf of the Shadow Proclamation

- **Protocol allows representatives to seize transport and technology, if required.**
- **The Shadow Proclamation has its own religious creed that includes a sole god.**

The Judoon are hired as enforcers and bodyguards. The muscle-bound creatures are perfect for situations that require a show of force.

ARCHITECT

The End of the Daleks

The Doctor is reluctant to take life, but his half-human, half-Time Lord incarnation has no qualms about destroying the whole Dalek race. He blasts the Dalekanium power feeds, annihilating the Daleks and their ship, and bringing an end to Davros and his designs on the universe.

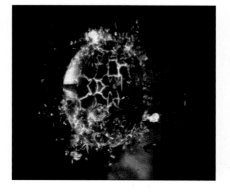

IRONSIDE
ONE

Painted khaki for
camouflage like
soldiers' fatigues

Suction cup is
used for fetching
files and carrying
tea trays

Ironsides

IT'S WORLD WAR II and London is the focus of a fierce bombing campaign known as the Blitz. War is pushing Britain to the brink of despair, but Professor Bracewell offers hope. He has invented robots with greater firepower than any other human-made weapon – the Ironsides. Destructive but obedient, they appear to be both the perfect soldier and the perfect servant. However, the Ironsides are hiding a dark secret but only the Doctor can see it.

The Perfect Warrior

Everyone except the Doctor thinks that the Ironsides are subservient robots, invented by Professor Bracewell. The deadly fighting machines offer assistance in any way they can – even serving cups of tea – and their deadly firepower is capable of blowing enemy aircraft out of the sky.

Secret Weapon

Deep below London's streets, Prime Minister Churchill and his advisors are in radio communication with people scattered along England's south coast, watching for imminent attack by Nazi aircraft. When they appear, Churchill uses Bracewell's Ironsides to exterminate them.

The Doctor pleads with Churchill to destroy the Ironsides. He is sure they will turn on humanity and try to destroy Earth. But Churchill will not give up his chance to end the war and ensure victory for Britain.

His famous "V" for Victory sign

Prime Minister Winston Churchill led Britain against Nazi Germany

1940s tailoring

IRONSIDE TWO

Union flag shows apparent alligience to Great Britain

Churchill's War

Although suspicious at first that the Ironsides are too good to be true, Churchill quickly sees the potential of these killing machines and is eager to harness their power. He is so desperate to save lives, that he would make a pact wth anyone. He simply cannot see a downside to these obedient robots.

Embodies the British Bulldog fighting spirit

Secrets and Schemes

Of course, the Doctor is right: the Ironsides are not loyal British soldiers, but are his oldest and deadliest enemy the Daleks. They have no conscience, no mercy and cannot be trusted. They are driven to destroy all that is not Dalek and their presence on Earth is all just an elaborate scheme to entrap the Doctor.

Ironsides have kit bags, just like soldiers

The subservience of the Ironsides doesn't fool the Doctor for a moment. In frustration he attacks one of them, and repeats his name and their true identity. Finally, the Ironsides reveal the truth: they are Daleks and they have been waiting for this testimony from the Doctor.

Professor Edwin Bracewell

Positronic brain full of ideas

Scottish scientist Professor Bracewell is extremely proud of his fearsome and loyal Ironsides, whom he believes will stop the war. He is stunned to discover that he didn't make them, and in fact they made him. He is simply an android implanted with false memories of another human's life.

An Ironside shoots Bracewell's left hand clean off, revealing Dalek technology under his human appearance.

Bracewell is powered by an Oblivion Continuum – a captured wormhole, that if detonated, would destroy the Earth.

The New Daleks

THE SCIENTIST

eye-stalk of the new true breed is the Dalek's organic eye, all squishy, blood-shot and alive!

THE SUPREME

MILLENNIA AGO, the Daleks seeded the universe with Progenitors, devices carrying the genetic make-up of the Daleks. Their creators lost track of them and the Progenitors became a legend. But in a crippled ship, three Daleks lived on with one of these mythical devices. However, the Doctor is the only one who can activate it. Once he falls into their trap, there is nothing he can do to prevent the resurrection of the Daleks.

Cleanse the Unclean!

In order to survive over the millennia, the three Daleks have become contaminated with other DNA and are no longer recognised as pure Dalek. Once they have engineered the new clean race of Daleks, they willingly submit to their extermination as nothing impure is tolerated by this terrible race.

Sucker tool is ideally suited to Dalek machinery, but can morph for other needs

THE ETERNAL

Dalek DNA stored inside

The Progenitor

Designed to store pure Dalek DNA, the Progenitor is the key to rebuilding the Dalek race and it can only be operated by Daleks. Because the Progenitor does not recognise the impure Daleks, they cannot activate it. Instead, they concoct a plan to use the Doctor's testimony that they are Daleks to unlock the machine and start the resurrection process.

Buttons on the ship's main central control panel are shaped to be operated by Dalek sucker tools.

Amy Saves the Day

The Oblivion Continuum in Professor Bracewell's android body is building up to explode and create a wormhole big enough to destroy the Earth. Only emotions can overpower his machine programming. Thanks to Amy's quick-thinking, he recalls the love he once felt for a woman called Dorabella. His humanity prevails and he deactivates.

Larger, reinforced Dalekanium casing houses superior organic creature

OBLIVION CONTINUUM CASING

Bonded polycarbide in Dalekanium now in bright colours

Improved scanning ability is not fooled by the TARDIS "self-destruct"

THE DRONE

Bracewell's ingenious gravity bubbles enable Spitfire planes to fly into space and attack the Dalek ship. The Daleks demand the attack be called off or Earth will be destroyed by the Oblivion Continuum that powers the professor. The Doctor won't let Earth die and so he allows the Daleks to flee to another time.

THE STRATEGIST

Restoration of the Daleks

A new super race of Daleks is born, led by the white Supreme Dalek. As yet, the Doctor doesn't know what this will mean for the future of the Dalek race but this much is certain: the universe is in terrible danger. From these five Daleks will grow a new Dalek army, vaster, deadlier and more cunning than ever. The Doctor has not seen the last of the Daleks.

Weeping Angels

The moment a Weeping Angel is seen, it turns into harmless stone.

WEEPING ANGELS ARE almost as old as the universe itself. They feed off potential energy by sending people into the past. Confined to history, their victims live out their lives, but in the present they are dead and the Angels feast on the days they might have had. The deadly Angels are quantum locked – they only exist when no-one can see them – and so they can never be killed.

Hands hide eyes, not tears

Angelic appearance disguises a killer

Sally Sparrow

When photographer Sally Sparrow breaks into the creepy old house Wester Drumlins to take some atmospheric pictures, she discovers the Weeping Angels. Many people have disappeared near the house, having fallen prey to the Angels. One of their victims is the Doctor, who is stranded in 1969 with Martha Jones.

Sally peels back the wallpaper to reveal a message from the Doctor – addressed to her! She's freaked out, but it takes more messages before she is ready to believe that someone is speaking to her from the past.

Kathy Nightingale

This is not the first time Sally has dragged her best friend, Kathy, into one of her schemes. Beneath her cheerful exterior, Kathy was actually lonely and longed for a new start. She gets her wish when she is zapped back to 1920, where she finds happiness with a new life in Hull and a husband called Ben.

The Grandson Paradox

Before Kathy died in 1987, she made her grandson Malcolm promise to deliver a letter to Sally at Wester Drumlins in 2007, explaining her disappearance. While he is doing so, the young Kathy is snatched out of time by the Angels – the event that will lead, ultimately, to Malcolm's birth.

Aged with time

KATHY'S LETTER

Weeping Angel Facts

• Because they are quantum locked, no-one knows what Weeping Angels look like in their natural, unfrozen state.
• The Angels are harmless while they are frozen in stone, but if their victim so much as blinks, they are set free to attack.
• The potential energy of the TARDIS could feed the Angels forever, but the power released would be enough to destroy the sun.
• The Angels move incredibly fast – they can cross a room in the blink of an eye, and that's only about 250 milliseconds!

The Angel's touch is deadly

The Angels are known as the Lonely Assassins – if an Angel ever looks at another of its kind, it will freeze, and if an Angel touches another, it will vanish into the past!

Billy Shipton

Billy Shipton, the policeman investigating the mysterious disappearances at Wester Drumlins, also falls prey to the Weeping Angels and finds himself in 1969, where the Doctor tracks him down. Billy then waits 38 years to deliver a message in person to Sally about the Doctor's plight.

Finds the Angels' victims by tracking disturbances in time

Parts scavenged from 1960s' machines

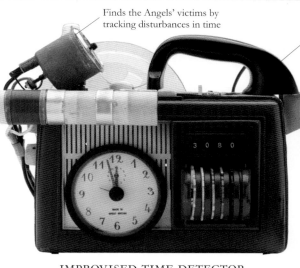

IMPROVISED TIME DETECTOR

Easter Eggs

In his new life in the past, Billy Shipton goes into DVD publishing and puts hidden tracks – Easter Eggs – on 17 DVDs. The recorded messages are for Sally and enable her to have a conversation with the Doctor across time.

The Doctor tricks the Angels. As the creatures surround the TARDIS, it dematerialises, leaving them staring at each other. Constantly observed, the Angels will remain stone forever.

With the help of Kathy's brother Larry, Sally compiles a folder of information for the Doctor. This completes the link so that, in his future, he will be able to communicate with her from the past.

Army of Angels

WEEPING ANGELS ARE THE most powerful, malevolent and deadly life form ever produced by evolution. The Doctor has met them before, but only a small group that was hiding out and weak. When the *Byzantium* space craft crashes, he meets another breed of Angels. They have been waiting a long time, but with a new energy source to feast on, they are beginning to restore themselves and soon will be a formidable army.

A lone Weeping Angel pulled from the ruins of Razbahan is being transported in the hold of the *Byzantium*. In induces a phase shift in the warp engines to crash the ship into a site full of hundreds of waiting Angels.

Amy and the Doctor encounter the Angels with River Song. She is on a mission to earn her pardon from prison while in the custody of a Bishop called Father Octavian.

Dinner Time

The crack in the universe like the one from Amy's bedroom is on the site of the crashed *Byzantium*. It is spilling temporal energy which the Angels plan to feed on. They think consuming it will give them dominion over all time and space. They do not realise that the power is so strong it will destroy them and wipe them from having ever existed.

Telepathically control ships's systems like light switches

Looking into the Angels' eyes is perilous

Serene faces mask violent intentions

Aplan Mortarium

The *Byzantium* lands on a temple with a network of catacombs built by the Aplan race called a Maze of the Dead or Mortarium. The Aplans fell prey to the Angels 400 years ago. Under the high-vaulted ceilings are weathered, broken statues that are actually starving Angels who are about to be fed.

There are no Weeping Angel pictures as they would be dangerous

The only book on the Weeping Angels

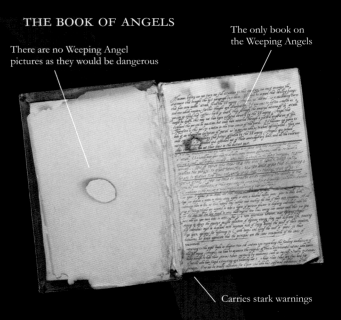

Carries stark warnings

The Book of Angels

This ancient book is a definitive work on the Angels, but it was dismissed as the ramblings of a mad man. It contains no pictures because that which holds the image of an Angel becomes itself an Angel.

51st Century Church

In 3,000 years, the Church becomes a military unit. Under Bishop Octavian, twenty armed Clerics are assigned to protect the Doctor and fight the Angels, but they are all killed by Angels or are wiped out by the crack in time.

Gun is useless against Weeping Angels

The Angels take over the *Byzantium's* systems, trapping those inside. The sonic screwdriver is no use at overriding the Angels' signals.

The Church is now an army

Weeping Angels Facts

Angel has not fed for centuries

- Weeping Angels can be patient for centuries. It doesn't mean that they're dormant or safe.
- Rather than displacing people in time like some Angels, these are more violent. They break humans' necks.
- Angels are able to strip the cerebral cortex from a person and reanimate a version of his or her consciousness in order to communicate with the Doctor.
- Angels are quantum-locked: they only exist when they're unseen. In the sight of any living creature, they cease to exist. It is a perfect evolutionary defence mechanism because it means they cannot be killed.
- As well as killing for the fun of it, Angels enjoy playing with people's emotions, inciting extra fear or anger.

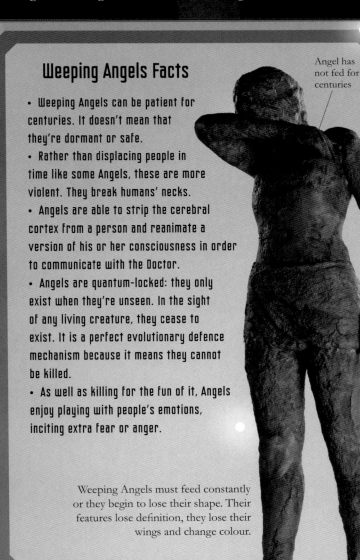

Weeping Angels must feed constantly or they begin to lose their shape. Their features lose definition, they lose their wings and change colour.

The Angel on the security footage advances on Amy and almost reaches her

00:11:27:19

Angel enters through Amy's eyes

Fatal Footage

Anything which holds the image of an Angel will become an Angel itself, so the three-second loop of security footage of the Angel in the hold is deadly. Amy freezes the recording on a blip at the end of the loop to render the Angel powerless.

When a person looks at something, it creates a mental image in their brain. In this way, an Angel establishes itself inside Amy's mind.

Angels Laughing

The Angels enjoy taunting the Doctor, playing with his guilt over Cleric Bob. He made Bob trust that he would keep him safe, but Bob was killed by the Angels. They revel in telling the Doctor that Bob died in fear

The Ood

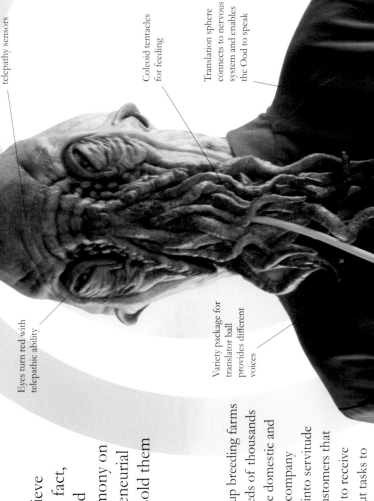

I N THE 42ND CENTURY, HUMANITY is led to believe that the Ood have only one purpose – to serve people. In fact, the Ood are not naturally subservient at all. A humanoid herd species, with squid-like tentacles, they lived in telepathic harmony on their planet, the Ood-Sphere, until the arrival of the entrepreneurial Halpen family. The tycoons enslaved the peaceful Ood and sold them throughout the Human Empire.

Bred to Serve

Ood Operations sets up breeding farms to produce the hundreds of thousands of Ood needed for the domestic and military markets. The company lobotomises the Ood into servitude and convinces their customers that the Ood's only goal is to receive orders and that without tasks to perform they would die.

Brainy Aliens

Natural Ood have two brains. Mostly they use the brain in their head, but memory and emotions are processed by the hind-brain, which is held in the peaceful Ood's hands. The Company replaces the hind-brain with a translator, which limits the Ood's telepathic ability and cuts them off from their communal Centre Brain.

Destroy the evidence! When the Ood regain the ability to think for themselves, ruthless company CEO Mr Halpen is prepared to wipe out every captive Ood in his factory complex in order to protect his reputation.

The Centre Brain

The telepathic Centre Brain connected the Ood in beautiful song for millennia, until Halpen's ancestors discovered it beneath the Ood-Sphere's Northern Glacier. It has been kept in captivity for 200 years.

Gloves worn for protection against machine solvents

Passive Ood see no reason to run away from their masters

Boots to keep balance on snow and ice

OOD SIGMA'S BELT

Belt is status symbol of executive slave

Supply of Ood-graft "tonic" administered to CEO Halpen

Single-dose cup for "tonic"

Dr Ryder   Ood Sigma

Friends of the Ood

After ten years of trying, Friends of the Ood activist Dr Ryder manages to infiltrate Ood Operations. As Head of Ood Management, he is able to reduce the dampening field around the telepathic Centre Brain, reconnecting the Ood so that the creatures can begin to think for themselves again.

Ood Facts

- There appear to be no male or female Ood, which suggests the species may be hermaphrodite.
- The Ood have no personal names but are given designations according to their functions, such as "Server Gamma 10".
- The Ood communicate through a low telepathic field rated as Basic 5. Basic 30 is the equivalent of screaming, and Basic 100 would result in brain death.
- Natural Ood do not kill. But as the processed Ood begin to experience emotions, the anger they feel leads them to use their translator spheres to destroy their oppressors.
- The Ood communicate through an endless song. When they are freed, the song goes out through the galaxies, calling all of Oodkind home.

Hind-brain gives Ood individuality

Ood Conversion

Seemingly faithful servant Ood Sigma has been providing Mr Halpen with "hair tonic" for ten years – but the drink is actually Ood-graft! Mr Halpen is turning into a natural Ood, and the release of the Centre Brain brings on his final transformation.

Cybermen

THEIR INVENTOR, John Lumic, believes Cybermen are the next stage of human evolution. He created these cybernetic creatures by bonding human brains within a strong steel shell. Cybermen are practically immortal, immensely strong and without emotion. With one mind, they form a vast silver army that marches relentlessly on, chanting, "Delete, delete, delete!"

Men of Steel

Cybermen may retain their human brains, but any human feelings are suppressed with an emotional inhibitor. They have an artifically grown nervous system that enables the brain to control their metal bodies and electronic parts. The steel armour is made up of a super-strong exterior shell (an exoskeleton) and a more flexible interior casing.

BACK VIEW

Voicebox

Cybus Industries logo can be removed to expose the emotional inhibitor

Exoskeleton increases upper body strength

Electrodes on hands deliver fatal electric shocks

Visual receptors

Fingertips with touch-sensitive pads

Super-strong armour protects the forearms

Chestplate shields the thermionic generator

Articulated armour for flexibility around lower torso

Coolant lines maintain low temperature inside the armour

Hip joint links exoskeleton to core armour

Cyberman Facts

- The Cybermen's armour is made from an extremely strong manganese-steel alloy.
- All Cybermen's brains are linked to form a single collective consciousness.
- The human brain inside the cyber-armour is stored at six degrees Celsius in a patented protein solution.
- Each Cyberman is powered by a thermionic generator.

CYBUS INDUSTRIES LOGO

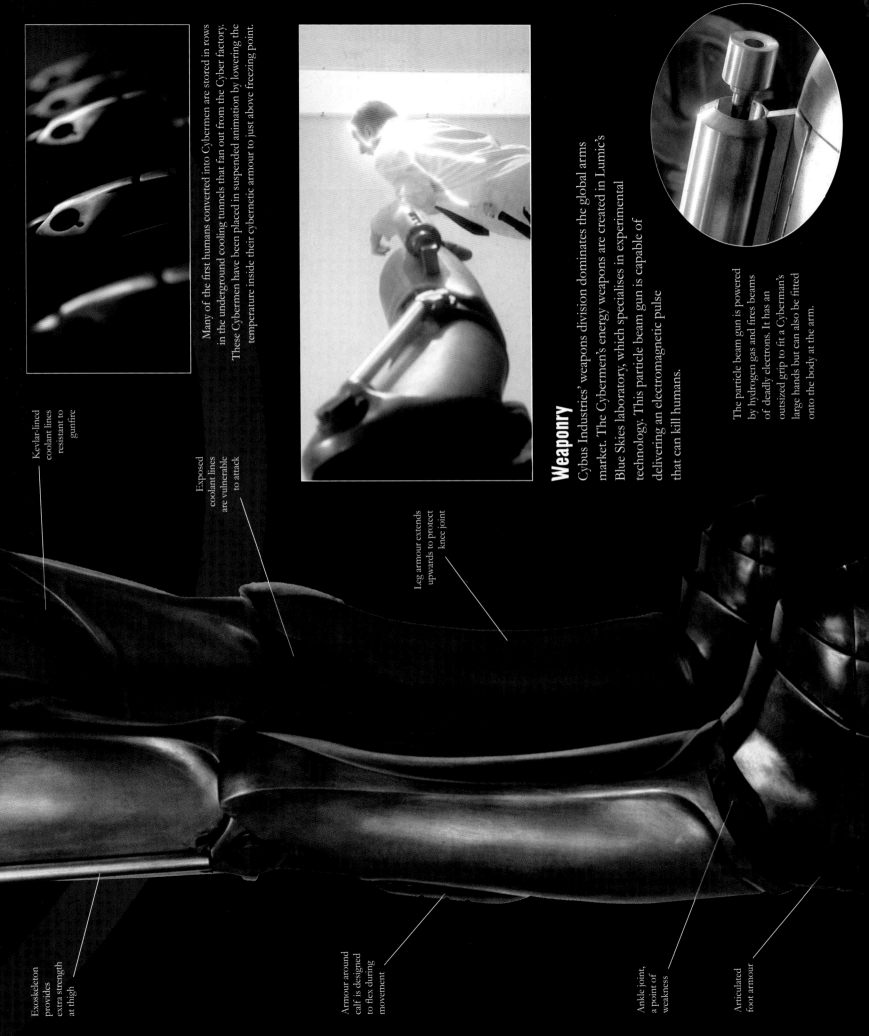

Many of the first humans converted into Cybermen are stored in rows in the underground cooling tunnels that fan out from the Cyber factory. These Cybermen have been placed in suspended animation by lowering the temperature inside their cybernetic armour to just above freezing point.

Weaponry

Cybus Industries' weapons division dominates the global arms market. The Cybermen's energy weapons are created in Lumic's Blue Skies laboratory, which specialises in experimental technology. This particle beam gun is capable of delivering an electromagnetic pulse that can kill humans.

The particle beam gun is powered by hydrogen gas and fires beams of deadly electrons. It has an outsized grip to fit a Cyberman's large hands but can also be fitted onto the body at the arm.

Kevlar-lined coolant lines resistant to gunfire

Exposed coolant lines are vulnerable to attack

Leg armour extends upwards to protect knee joint

Exoskeleton provides extra strength at thigh

Armour around calf is designed to flex during movement

Ankle joint, a point of weakness

Articulated foot armour

Cybus Industries

W HEN THE TARDIS crashes on a parallel Earth, the Doctor and his companions find a world similar to their own but dominated by one organisation, Cybus Industries. This massive business empire controls the world's media, finance, property, communications and technology. Its mega-rich but dying leader, John Lumic, has secretly spent years and millions of pounds researching an end to human mortality. His plan is to "upgrade" humanity, turning it into a race of immortal Cybermen.

John Lumic

The founder of Cybus Industries, John Lumic, is a scientific genius whose inventions have made him the most powerful man on Earth. But he suffers from a terrible wasting disease that has confined him to a wheelchair and will ultimately kill him. Power and the fear of death have turned him into an insane megalomaniac who sees mortality as the ultimate enemy. To him, humanity and individuality are expendable in the search for an end to death.

Air Ship

With crime rampant on the streets of Britain and a night-time curfew in place, Britain's wealthy elite has taken to living in giant air ships floating above London. These zeppelins are manufactured by Cybus Industries, whose leader, John Lumic, has his own luxury model. He can send signals to people's EarPods via a transmitter on his ship.

Satellite transmitter

Bow reinforced to withstand headwinds

EarPod transmitter

Rigid hull, made from a light aluminium alloy

Horizontal fin for stability

Starboard propeller

Ventral fin

Spotlights, used when landing airship in darkness

Bridge at front of gondola

Gondola with accommodation and facilities for passengers and crew

Port propeller for forward thrust

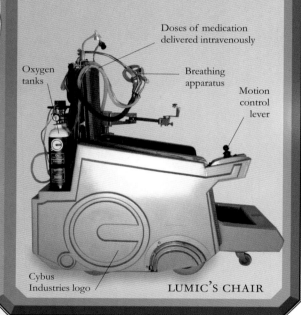

Doses of medication delivered intravenously

Oxygen tanks

Breathing apparatus

Motion control lever

Cybus Industries logo

LUMIC'S CHAIR

On this parallel Earth, everyone wears an EarPod. Developed by Cybus Industries, these sophisticated communications devices download news and entertainment directly into the user's brain and exert a form of mind control.

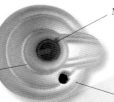

EARPOD

Microwave antenna

Earpiece shaped like Cybus Industries logo

Durable plastic polymer coating

The Cybus Factory

Lumic secretly converts the disused buildings at Battersea Power Station in London into a factory for creating Cybermen. This is just one of many similar factories around the world. As Lumic attempts to perfect his cyber-conversion techniques, many of London's homeless people are abducted and experimented on. Inside the factory, there are hundreds of cylindrical conversion chambers. Each chamber is designed to transform a human into a Cyberman in less than a minute. The factory is capable of converting thousands of people a day into emotionless Cybermen.

The brain is the only part of a human that survives inside a Cyberman. Lumic has to find a way to remove the human brain without killing it. He realises that speed is vital. With pain receptors in the brain deactivated by EarPods, the powerful cutting gear cuts open the human skull, carves out the brain and transfers it into its new metal home in seconds. The remaining body is simply incinerated.

A Cyberman's human brain is housed in its steel helmet. Once in place, the brain is flooded with a chilled protein solution that preserves and nurtures it, eliminating cellular decay.

The Cyber Controller

When John Lumic is transformed into the Cyber Controller, he retains the emotions of anger and hatred, and his voicebox mimics Lumic's actual voice. The Cyber Controller is physically connected to a Cyber Throne. From there, he is able to control the activity of all the Cybermen.

Data carried along a series of fibreoptic cables

Coolant fed into Cyber Controller's body

Transparent brain-case

Throne constructed from titanium alloy

Steel body armour

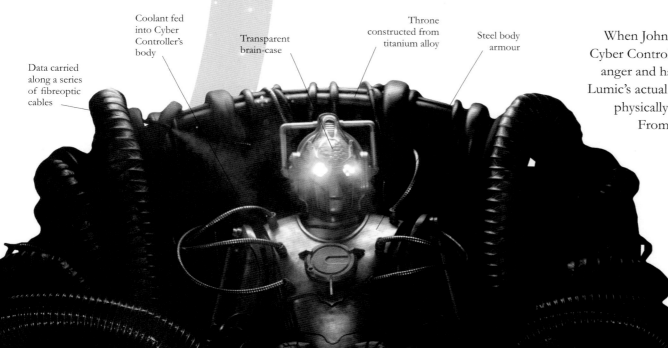

The emotional inhibitor removes a Cyberman's human feelings. Without it, the Cyberman will go insane.

When the emotional inhibitors are deactivated, the Cybermen are killed by the mental trauma.

Human brain
visible inside
Cybercasing

Distinctive
black visor

Cyberleader is
capable of lying
to gain advantage

The CyberKing

W HEN THE CYBERMEN were sucked into the
Void during the Battle of Canary Wharf, the Doctor
thought he had seen the end of them. But a few
survived and broke back into the world, using a time-
travelling Dimension Vault stolen from the Daleks.
They arrived in London in December 1851 and set
about their business of abduction, murder and
creating the CyberKing – a giant battleship to lead
their invasion of Earth and the conversion of
the human population into Cybermen.

Mask and metal
hands are the only
visible non-organic
parts

The Cyberleader

Taking direct control of Cyberforces is the
Cyberleader. He is easily distinguished from
his all-silver troops by the black details on
his helmet. The Cyber-race has only one
Cyberleader. If its body is destroyed then its
knowledge and functions are downloaded
into another Cyberman whose body is
upgraded. If this is not immediately possible,
the Cyberleader's program is beamed back
to a control computer and stored.

CyberKing Facts

• The Cyberleader is in charge of overseeing the plans to
build the CyberKing, which will aid their invasion of Earth.
• The CyberKing is a vast, dreadnought-class battleship,
200 feet tall and fashioned in the rough shape of a
Cyberman.
• Inside the CyberKing's chest is a Cyber-conversion unit,
capable of transforming millions of humans and other
organic life forms into Cybermen.
• The CyberKing runs on electricity.
In order to generate electricity in Victorian
London, the Cybermen use coal,
which is shovelled by armies
of workhouse children.

The CyberKing dwarfs any structure on Earth and wreaks
devastation with a giant laser blaster on one arm and mortar
launcher on the other.

Miss Hartigan

Mercy Hartigan, Matron of the St Joseph's workhouse, deeply resents the men who oppress womankind. She accepts the Cybermen's offer of liberation, not realising they plan to liberate her from her feelings by incorporating her into the CyberKing. But strong-minded Mercy is a match for the metal monsters. Her Cybermind retains emotions and bends the Cybermen to her will, combining their logic and strength with her fury and passion.

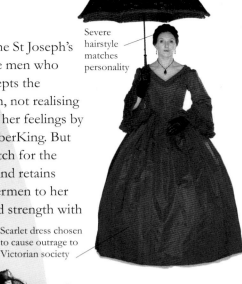

Severe hairstyle matches personality

Scarlet dress chosen to cause outrage to Victorian society

Metal "ears" transmit audio data

Creature can hiss but not form words

The Other Doctor

After Jackson Lake's wife is killed by the Cybermen, he wants to forget. He finds an infostamp – a steel object for storing compressed data – but it backfires and streams facts about the Doctor into his head, causing him to believe that he is the Time Lord. But Lake's courage and ingenuity are genuine and gain him a companion – brave and resourceful servant Rosita Farisi who throws in her lot with him when he saves her life.

Rosita becomes nursemaid to Jackson's motherless son

Victorian gentleman's outfit – a style also once favoured by the real Doctor

Not only does Jackson Lake believe he is the Doctor, he also calls his screwdriver a sonic screwdriver and builds a TARDIS – a hot air balloon he names a "Tethered Aerial Release Developed In Style".

JACKSON LAKE   ROSITA FARISI

Cybershades

The Cybermen's latest innovation, the Cybershade, is created by placing the brain of a primitive creature, such as a cat or dog, inside a cybernetic form instead of the usual human. These Shades have less intelligence than their Cybermasters, but possess the speed and agility that Cybermen lack. They are able to outrun humans and scale vertical surfaces. Shades act like hounds to the Cybermen's huntsmen, tracking and rounding up prey.

Flexible Cyberfingers

CYBERSHADE

Creature scuttles on all-fours

The conversion of animals into Cybershades requires less power than producing full Cybermen. They act as the Cybermen's eyes and ears in London, providing visual and audio data, while allowing the remaining Cybermen to concentrate their resources on preparing the CyberKing factory and battleship.

Platform One

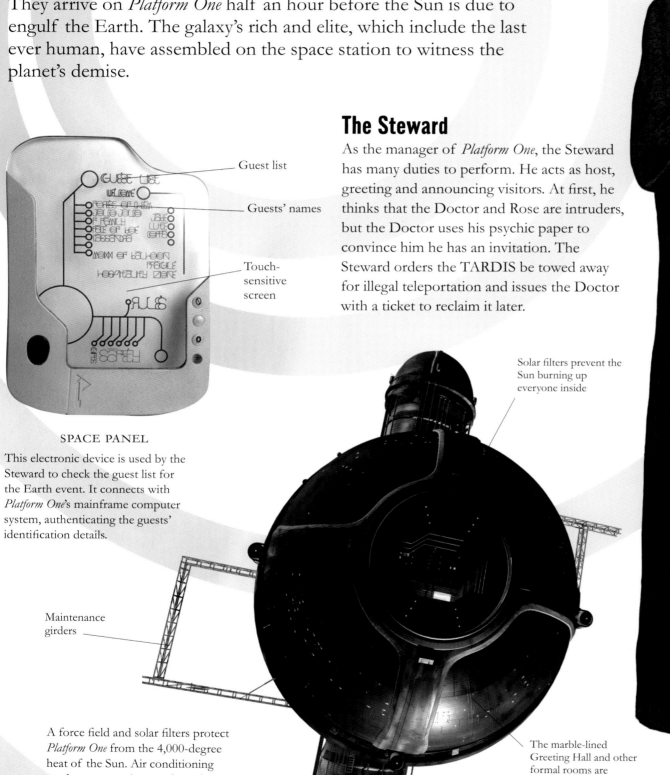

WHEN ROSE CHOOSES the future for her first trip in the TARDIS, the Doctor shows off his time-travelling skills by taking her to the year 5.5/Apple/26, five billion years in the future. They arrive on *Platform One* half an hour before the Sun is due to engulf the Earth. The galaxy's rich and elite, which include the last ever human, have assembled on the space station to witness the planet's demise.

The Steward is a blue-skinned humanoid

He wears a formal robe of welcome

The Steward

As the manager of *Platform One*, the Steward has many duties to perform. He acts as host, greeting and announcing visitors. At first, he thinks that the Doctor and Rose are intruders, but the Doctor uses his psychic paper to convince him he has an invitation. The Steward orders the TARDIS be towed away for illegal teleportation and issues the Doctor with a ticket to reclaim it later.

Guest list

Guests' names

Touch-sensitive screen

SPACE PANEL

This electronic device is used by the Steward to check the guest list for the Earth event. It connects with *Platform One*'s mainframe computer system, authenticating the guests' identification details.

Solar filters prevent the Sun burning up everyone inside

Maintenance girders

A force field and solar filters protect *Platform One* from the 4,000-degree heat of the Sun. Air conditioning on the space station regulates the temperature inside. All the systems are automatic, run by a huge fan-cooled computer mainframe.

The marble-lined Greeting Hall and other formal rooms are situated in the disc-shaped hub

Communications sensors

Swept up "birds' nest" hairstyle is adorned with leaves

To show her status, Jabe wears a luxurious robe with a jewel-encrusted collar

Out of courtesy, Jabe keeps her liana, a vine-like appendage, out of sight

Helmet and visor for protection

Rose sees the Earth from space for the first time

Small blue-skinned aliens work as guards

The Sun had been threatening to swallow the Earth for years, but the planet was saved by the National Trust. It used gravity satellites to stop the Sun's expansion and restored the planet to its former glory. But when the Trust's money ran out, the Earth was evacuated and left to die.

Dignitaries from the Forest of Cheem

Ceremonial armour of lacquered paper

Official robes, made of woven paper and gold thread

Thousands of blue-skinned humanoid aliens work on *Platform One*. One of them, a plumber called Raffalo, tells Rose that she is from Crespallion, which is part of the Jaggit Brocade, affiliated to the Scarlet Junction, in the Convex 56. This makes Rose realise how far away from home she is.

PLATFORM GUARD

The Trees from the Forest of Cheem are an arboreal species descended from the tropical rainforests on Earth. They are highly intelligent and have deep respect for all life forms. As the owners of vast amounts of land and forests on many planets, they have great wealth and influence.

COFFA AND LUTE, JABE'S COMPANIONS

Jabe, the Walking Tree

A seven-foot-tall alien, Jabe is the leader of the Trees, visitors from the Forest of Cheem. This noble, woody creature's full name is Jabe Ceth Ceth Jafe. Her scanning device reveals the Doctor's true identity, and she sympathises with his plight as the last Time Lord.

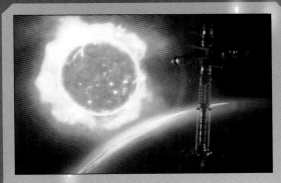

Platform One Facts

- The station is an observation platform that travels between stars.
- The galaxy's elite pay to watch artistic events on the luxury space station.
- It is owned by a vast intergalactic corporation, which employs the Steward.
- Like many items on the station, the exo-glass in the viewscreens is capable of self-repair.
- Teleportation, religion and all forms of weapons are forbidden on *Platform One*.

Guests of *Platform One*

THE STRICTLY INVITATION-ONLY event on *Platform One* is reserved for the galaxy's wealthy elite. The honoured guests, from many different worlds and a variety of races and species, have all come to pay their last respects to Earth – and to network with the universe's most influential beings.

Chain of rank

THE ADHERENTS OF THE REPEATED MEME

The faceless, black-robed Adherents are greeted as guests on *Platform One*. But they are really remotely operated droids controlled by Lady Cassandra. Their gifts of metal spheres contain sabotaging robot spiders.

Tough metal exoskeleton

Vision sensor

ROBOT SPIDER

Scuttling out of the metal spheres, the "spiders" are programmed to sabotage the *Platform One* computer, lift the sun filters and destroy the space station.

THE FACE OF BOE

The sponsor of the *Platform One* event is a huge humanoid head called the Face of Boe. He is the last of Boekind and, at millions of years old, the oldest being in the Isop galaxy. Boe's head is kept in a huge jar, and instead of hair, he has tendrils that end in small pods. This influential alien is one of the few survivors of the *Platform One* disaster.

Thick, leathery reptile skin

Thick fur cloaks

THE BROTHERS HOP PYLEEN

These two wealthy lizard brothers are from the clifftops of Rex Vox. The pair made their fortune by inventing Hyposlip Travel Systems. They favour fur clothes, which keep their cold-blooded bodies warm.

Large four-fingered hands with sharp nails

THE AMBASSADORS OF THE CITY STATE OF BINDING LIGHT

Due to their race's oxygen sensitivity, oxygen levels must be monitored strictly at all times in the Ambassadors' presence.

A special mix of air is pumped into the face masks

CAL "SPARKPLUG"

The cybernetic hyperstar Cal "Sparkplug" MacNannovich arrives with his "plus-one".

Huge feathered head

MR AND MRS PAKOO

These bird-like creatures may be husband and wife but it is impossible to tell who is who. The pair have huge eyes and vicious-looking beaks. Their feathered heads give away their avian origins, although they walk like humans.

THE MOXX OF BALHOON

This goblin-like creature's legs are crippled by disease. He travels around on a speedy anti-gravity chair that contains a servo-motor. This device replaces his bodily fluids every 20 minutes because otherwise he sweats dangerous glaxic acid. The Moxx greets visitors with formal spitting.

Lady Cassandra

THE LAST "PURE" HUMAN, Lady Cassandra O'Brien Dot Delta Seventeen, is the only human who hasn't interbred with other species. Being incredibly beautiful in the past, Cassandra was adored by everyone. Now, her desire to keep thin and wrinkle-free means she is prepared to murder the guests on *Platform One* and cash in on the insurance money to pay for more operations.

Lipstick and skin are all that are left of Cassandra's body

Cassandra gives this rare ostrich egg to the Steward. It actually contains a teleportation field that Cassandra uses to escape, temporarily, from *Platform One*. She also secretly controls the Adherents of the Repeated Meme.

The ostrich is an extinct fire-breathing beast from Earth

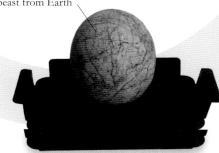

CASSANDRA'S "GIFT"

Without moisturisation, her skin would dry out and disintegrate

Metal frame connects nerve fibres to Cassandra's brain

Skin Deep

After 708 plastic surgery operations, Cassandra is finally as thin as she always wanted to be. Reduced to a translucent piece of skin with eyes and a mouth stretched across a frame, she is still obsessed with her looks. Rose is repulsed by her shallowness, calling her "the bitchy trampoline".

Brain kept in a jar of preserving solution

Lady Cassandra was thought to have died on *Platform One*, but her faithful servant, a forced-growth clone called Chip, hides her in a hospital on New Earth. With access to medicine and supplies, he cares for her while spider robots search for a new body.

Cassandra's personal assistants are always close by, ready to spray her with a scientifically patented moisturising formula.

Magnification goggles for seeing the tiniest wrinkle

Gloves and masks protect Cassandra from germs

Moisturisation formula canister

Canisters can be filled with acid and used as weapons

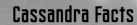

Cassandra Facts

- Cassandra's "pure" human parents were the last to be buried in Earth's soil.
- She was born an American male but was transformed into an English woman.
- She has been married several times.
- Although her "body" was destroyed in the *Platform One* disaster, her brain survived.

The Slitheen

THE LUSH, ABUNDANT planet of Raxacoricofallapatorius, on the edge of the Milky Way, is home to a species of green-skinned, calcium-based bipedals. While most Raxacoricofallapatorians are peaceful and law-abiding, one particular family's criminality has given the entire species a bad reputation: the Slitheen clan. Banished from their own star system, the Slitheen now terrorise other worlds – including Earth.

Well-adapted Lifeforms

Raxacoricofallapatorians are well suited to life on their own planet, using their powerful arms to swim from island to island in the great burgundy oceans and piercing through blizzards at the four poles with their large eyes.

The Slitheen family thinks nothing of profiting from planetary war. On Earth, family members stage the crash-landing of a spaceship in order to kick-start a nuclear war and turn the planet into radioactive slag, which can be sold in other galaxies as spaceship fuel.

Second Skins

As wanted criminals on many worlds, the Slitheen are often forced to work in disguise. Earth-based family members use compression field-generating neck collars to squeeze their huge bulks into the empty skin vessels of their human victims.

The Slitheen fitted their human costumes with zips, hidden under hairlines or hats. Unzipping produces a burst of contained compression energy.

The Slitheen find human skins cramped, preferring their "naked" form.

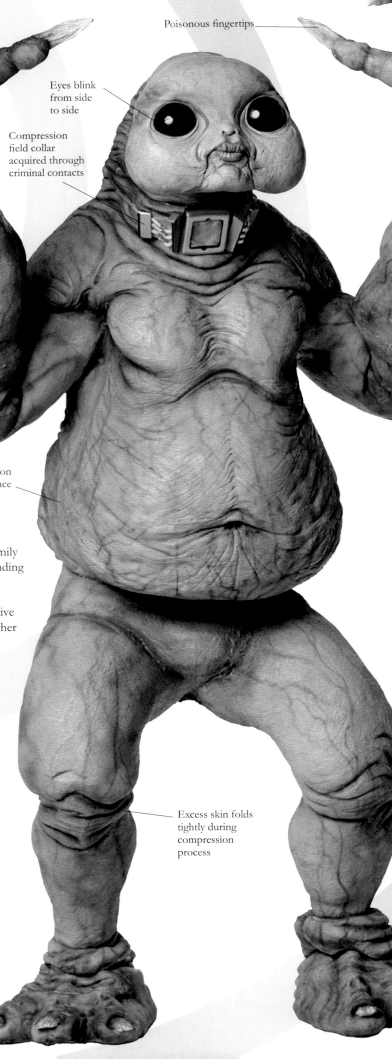

Poisonous fingertips

Eyes blink from side to side

Compression field collar acquired through criminal contacts

Auxiliary tendons support long arms

Gas exchange during compression causes painful flatulence

Excess skin folds tightly during compression process

Raxacoricofallapatorian Facts

- Raxacoricofallapatorian society is organised entirely around its large, powerful families. Family members use the species' extraordinary sense of smell to locate each other across vast distances and even to sense the death of loved ones.
- Raxacoricofallapatorian family names are a complex affair, with any number of hyphenations expressing the exact branch and sub-branch of complicated family trees.
- The Slitheen is one of the planet's oldest families, tracing its line back to the legendary Huspick Degenerate scion, who controlled an illegal spice-smuggling organisation.
- Raxacoricofallapatorians hatch from eggs (*shown right*), using their powerful claws to break through the shell.

1. Faced with a murderous Slitheen on Earth, Jackie throws vinegar at it....

2. The acid in the vinegar reacts with the calcium in the Slitheen's body....

3. The resulting explosive reaction causes instant annihilation.

Fatal Weakness

Raxacoricofallapatorians' living-calcium structure is highly vulnerable to certain substances, most dangerously acetic acid, which almost always causes a fatal explosive reaction. On their home planet, the most heinous criminals were executed by being lowered into vats of acetic acid, ensuring a slow, painful death.

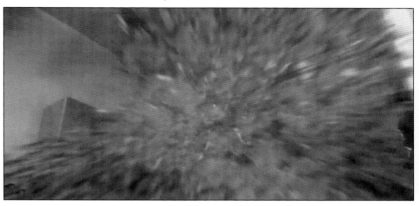

Unwitting Target

The closeness of the Slitheen clan is its undoing when all the Earth-based members hold a triumphant family gathering in 10 Downing Street. Given a single, reasonably contained target, the Doctor decides to risk launching a Harpoon missile.

Panic ensues in the Slitheen family's final moments.

The Abzorbaloff

Originating on Raxacoricofallapatorius's sister planet Clom, the creature known as the Abzorbaloff can absorb other creatures in order to steal their knowledge and consciousnesses. The process is highly unstable and requires a limitation field device to avoid the remnants of the most recently absorbed victims pulling him apart from the inside.

Cane contains limitation field that stops Abzorbaloff being absorbed himself by trapped consciousnesses

Faces of absorbed victims remain visible in flesh

The Slitheen impersonating Margaret Blaine of MI5 broke rank with the family and teleported away from the Downing Street blast using a teleporter device hidden in her earrings. She vowed revenge on the miserable human race.

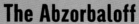

Satellite 5

ORBITING EARTH in the year 200,000, the Satellite 5 space station is the planet's largest media hub. Replacing all earlier broadcast satellites, it transmits news and entertainment throughout the Fourth Great and Bountiful Human Empire. The space station is also home to thousands of human employees, including journalists, who collect the news remotely via neural implants, and the Editor, who oversees them. Also onboard is the Jagrafess, a gigantic slug-like alien, who secretly manipulates the news in order to turn humans into slaves.

In a media centre on Satellite 5, journalists use the chips in their heads to gather news stories from across the Empire. They send the news via data hand plates to Cathica, a journalist implanted with an infospike. She lies on an infochair and processes the news before transmitting it to the Empire. However, unknown to the journalists, the news is really going to the Jagrafess for editing before transmission.

The mysterious Editor manages the space station from Floor 500. Unseen and unknown, the Editor monitors the journalists' thoughts via the chips in their heads. He was appointed by a consortium of interstellar banks, who installed the Jagrafess to profit from humanity's enslavement. The Editor is a pale, softly spoken human and utterly ruthless.

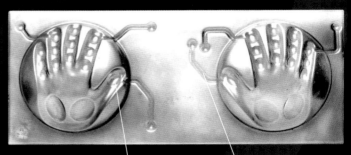

Biogenetic analyser   Data defragmenter

HAND PLATES

CLIPBOARD

- Media centre seating system
- Clipboard's infopaper displays data

Chip inside interfaces with pay stations

Stick is used like a credit card

Stick can be topped up with currency at credit terminals

CURRENCY STICK

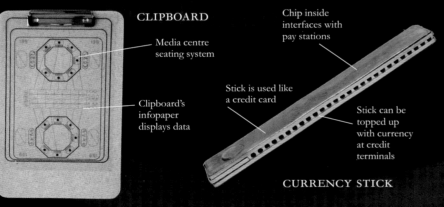

An infospike is a portal in the forehead that connects the brain to Satellite 5's computers. The infospike opens with a click of the fingers and connects to the computers via spheres of energy in the media centres. Using the currency stick the Doctor has given him, Adam pays to have an infospike installed.

The Freedom Foundation

The Freedom Foundation is a group of 15 humans who discover Satellite 5's manipulation of humanity and are determined to stop it.

One by one, the 15 Freedom Foundation members have been eliminated. The last surviving member, Suki Macrae Cantrell, infiltrated Satellite 5. On Floor 500, she pulled a gun on the Editor, but she was killed by the station's real boss, the Jagrafess.

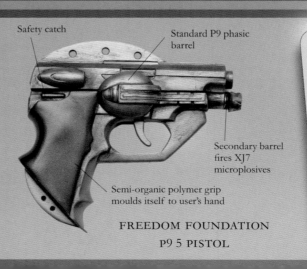

Safety catch

Standard P9 phasic barrel

Secondary barrel fires XJ7 microplosives

Semi-organic polymer grip moulds itself to user's hand

FREEDOM FOUNDATION P9 5 PISTOL

Freedom Foundation Manifesto

- Closure of Satellite 5
- Full investigation into Satellite 5's activities
- No individual to own more than 3 media outlets
- Freezing of the assets of Satellite 5's backers

Space Station

Satellite 5 functions as a
regular working media hub –
except for one section, which has
been secretly modified to accommodate
a highly unusual occupant: the Jagrafess.
This gigantic creature lives on Floor 500,
the topmost floor of the orbital platform.
Since the Jagrafess's fast metabolism
produces massive amounts of heat, a
secondary ventilation system and auxiliary
heat sinks were introduced to vent heat away
from Floor 500. This has resulted in the top
floor icing up like an Arctic winter, while the
floors below are unbearably hot.

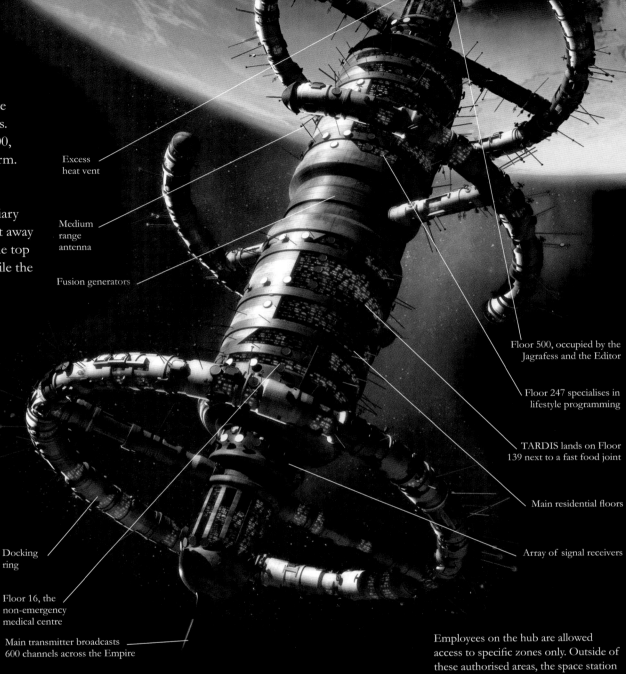

Excess
heat vent

Medium
range
antenna

Fusion generators

Floor 500, occupied by the
Jagrafess and the Editor

Floor 247 specialises in
lifestyle programming

TARDIS lands on Floor
139 next to a fast food joint

Main residential floors

Array of signal receivers

Docking
ring

Floor 16, the
non-emergency
medical centre

Main transmitter broadcasts
600 channels across the Empire

The Jagrafess's full name is the
Mighty Jagrafess of the Holy Hadrojassic
Maxarodenfoe. The Editor calls him
Max for short. This monstrous, slimy
alien with razor-sharp teeth is the true
ruler of the Empire.

Employees on the hub are allowed
access to specific zones only. Outside of
these authorised areas, the space station
is a mystery and the overall layout can
only be speculative.

Holographic
screens monitor
Satellite 5
activity

Keyboard
for manual
entry

Chairs for
the drones
who operate
the terminals

Floor 500 media centre

Floor 500

Everyone who works on Satellite 5 wants to be promoted
and transferred up to Floor 500. However, those who
make it to the top floor don't live long. Killed by the
Jagrafess, they work on as his drones – puppets
controlled by the chip in their heads – until their bodies
wear out. Floor 500 media centre is the control room of
Satellite 5, where the Editor and the drones monitor all
human activity on the space station.

The Sycorax

THESE SKINLESS HUMANOIDS inhabit a barren asteroid named the Fire Trap from the JX82 system. Consisting of many warlike tribes, the Sycorax fight with swords, whips and their own school of magic spells and curses. To survive, these interstellar scavengers ransack other planets. One tribe, the Halvinor, crash through Earth's atmosphere, planning to steal its land and minerals, but don't anticipate encountering the regenerating Doctor when he takes Rose home for Christmas.

The Sycorax adhere to traditions of honourable combat and will never turn down a challenge.

Sycorax Ship Facts

- The Sycorax ship is an asteroid fitted with engines. When an alien ship collided with their asteroid, the Sycorax used the alien technology to add powerful engines.
- Many more asteroids have since been converted by the Sycorax, with each tribe claiming their own. These asteroid ships are used to raid other planets for food and resources.
- The Sycorax ship that attacked Earth was driven by an All Speed Inter-System Type K engine.

Sycorax Great Hall

This enormous hall was hollowed out of the Fire Trap's core many centuries ago. Its primitive structure is combined with space-age technology, such as a teleporter to travel on and off the ship. The hall is used for tribal meetings and the hole in the roof allows solar and lunar light for ancient Sycorax rituals.

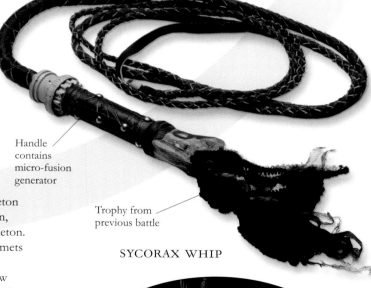

Thong conducts huge energies

Handle contains micro-fusion generator

Trophy from previous battle

SYCORAX WHIP

Part of the Sycorax skeleton is located outside the skin, forming a partial exoskeleton. Their fearsome bone helmets are worn over the top to protect the vulnerable raw skin and muscle underneath.

The Sycorax whip, when used on a human body, instantly destroys all the atoms of human flesh, so that only a pile of charred bones remains. This devastating effect is seen on the prime minister's aide, scientist Daniel Llewelyn.

Claw of pet Razorback

Fearsome bone helmet

Blood mane from leader's first kill

Trophies of conquered species

Red robe signifies high rank

Sycorax Leader

Sycorax live for 400 years and it took two and half centuries for the Sycorax Leader to become head of his people – the Halvinor tribe. He rose through the ranks by various trials of strength and combat.

The Sycorax will conquer a world by any means. When an Earth probe containing A+ human blood crashes into their ship, they feed it into a control matrix and enslave everyone on Earth who has A+ blood.

The Doctor challenges the Sycorax Leader to single combat for the fate of Earth. Honour bound to accept, he is defeated by the Time Lord and the Sycorax agree to leave humanity alone.

Forearm guards

Plumage of Courage

Pommel embedded with precious stones

Judoon-skin belt

Lanyard of the order of Prokraxis

Barbed handle

Protective Baltaric spats

Blade forged from Samavagem

SYCORAX SWORD

Fluted cap worn by all Sisters

The Sisters can tell each other apart by their scent and the colour of their fur

The eldest in her litter, Matron Casp grew up used to getting her own way

MATRON CASP

New Earth

STANDING ON *PLATFORM ONE* in the year five billion, the Doctor and Rose had watched the Sun expand and obliterate the Earth. However, Earth's destruction inspired revivalists to search for a similar world. Twenty years later and 50,000 light years away in galaxy M87, the ideal place was found and named New Earth. The Doctor takes Rose there in the year 5,000,000,023, and visits again with Martha 30 years later.

Dazzling New New York – the fifteenth since the United States' original – is New Earth's major city. It is ruled by the Senate, who live in the gleaming Overcity, while the poorer citizens live in the grim Undercity below.

MEDICAL SCANNER

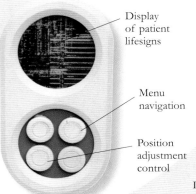

Display of patient lifesigns

Menu navigation

Position adjustment control

Prestigious Hospital

In 5,000,000,023, a hospital commands an imposing coastal position on New Earth. Its gleaming, sterile wards are sealed from the outside air to prevent contamination. Visitors to the wards are automatically disinfected when they enter the building's lifts.

Sisters of Plenitude

The hospital is run by the humanoid feline Sisters of Plenitude. They specialise in treating incurable diseases – their reputation for almost-miraculous cures is well-known. The Order is as single-minded about its mission to cure patients as it is fiercely secretive about its treatment methods.

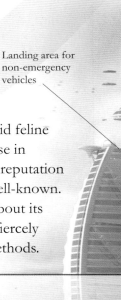

Universal symbol for hospital

Ambulance landing bay

Landing area for non-emergency vehicles

Human Farm

Deep in the basement of the hospital is the secret of the Sisters' healing powers. Human clones are infected with every known disease and experimented on to find new cures. When the Doctor and Rose discover the clones are sentient, they free them, and a new human species is born.

Life on the Motorway

By the time the Doctor returns in 5,000,000,053, life in New New York has drastically changed. Many denizens of the Undercity have set off on the Motorway, dreaming of a better life higher up. This highway is 20 lanes across and 50 lanes deep. Its traffic moves five miles every 12 years, but is going nowhere because the exit has been sealed to protect it from danger above.

Self-replicating fuel, muscle stimulants for exercise and waste products recycled as food mean no one has to leave their car. Even babies are born on board – Valerie and Thomas Kincade Brannigan's litter of kittens are Children of the Motorway, and have never known any other way of life.

Communicator used to call cars on the driver's Friends List

Fur is turning grey with age

Kitten nursery, equipped for the babies' every need

Novice Hame

Catperson Novice Hame nurses the Face of Boe as penance for the clone experiments. When a virus kills everyone in the Overcity, the Face of Boe hastily seals the Undercity, and uses his life-force to keep it running for 24 lonely years. When the Doctor arrives, he rescues the Undercity population, so they can reinhabit New New York.

Teleportation device, also controls external lights

NOVICE HAME'S BRACELET

Holographic presenter Sally Calypso's fabricated broadcasts convince the Motorway residents that all is normal in New New York.

Carries gun in case of Motorway pirates

Macra

The giant, crab-like Macra were once the scourge of galaxy M87. They forced humans to mine the poisonous gas they fed on. Over billions of years they devolved into simple beasts and were kept in the New New York Zoo. Escaped specimens have bred and thrive beneath the smog-shrouded Motorway, hunting its travellers.

The airborne virus that killed everyone in the Overcity mutated from the popular mood-changing drug, Bliss.

NOVICE HAME

The Werewolf

QUEEN VICTORIA suffered several attempts on her life, but none so bizarre as that of a power-hungry alien parasite that sought to infect her body in order to take over England for its own ends — perhaps even to steal Victorian technology to carve out its own vast, steam-powered empire in space! Able to change into werewolf form, this alien has bewitched the monks of a remote, Scottish monastery and plans to use them to hatch its deadly plot against the Queen.

The Torchwood Estate is a place of legend and mystery. Its very name is said to derive from the wood of a lightning-struck gallows — torched wood — used in its construction. Wild rumours were further stoked in the 1800s when the house's eccentric owner, Sir George MacLeish, built a gigantic rooftop observatory.

Chance Encounter

Landing in Scotland in 1879, the Doctor meets Queen Victoria on her way to Balmoral Castle. Unable to resist the opportunity to make the acquaintance of an English monarch, the Doctor uses his psychic paper to supply him with credentials to tag along to Torchwood House, where the Queen intends to spend the night.

Fighting staff made of a rare wood that grows in the area

Mistletoe worn around neck under robe

Habit conceals orange fighting robes

Bedevilled Brethren

Near Torchwood stands the monastery of St Catherine's Glen. The monks, led by the crazed Father Angelo, are guardians of a powerful secret — they worship an alien being that fell to Earth close to their monastery in the 1500s. The alien survives by infecting human hosts.

Before the Queen and the Doctor arrive at Torchwood, the monks take over the house, overpowering the staff with unnaturally fast fighting techniques.

Informed of Queen Victoria's movements by the monks, and desperate to infect itself into a being of real power, the alien commands the monks to transport it — in its human host — to Torchwood House. Now, all it needs is for the full moon to provide the power to transform it to its werewolf form.

Sharp claws rip prey apart

To a seasoned space-time traveller like Rose, the young prisoner's eyes betray the unmistakable presence of a life form that is not from Earth.

Mistletoe headbands used to ward off the Werewolf

Super-sensitive ears

Inhuman eyes betray alien presence inside

Royal Secrets

Official records remain silent on the strange events at the Torchwood Estate. Yet it is perhaps no coincidence that shortly afterwards, Queen Victoria secretly established the Torchwood Institute to research and fight Britain's enemies "beyond imagination".

Wrist suffers mysterious cut in struggle with werewolf

Official emblem of state

ROYAL ATTACHE CASE

Sharp teeth rip apart flesh

Thick skin deflects bullets

Powerful hind legs allow short bursts of fast running or jumping

When the Doctor discovers a telescope with an unusual array of prisms and learns that the current owner, Sir Robert, is obsessed with werewolf legends and the heavens, he speculates that the telescope might have a secret function.

Objective lens cell

Tube ring

Focusing knob

Eyepiece

CENTRAL TUBE OF TELESCOPE

Alien Being

To locals, the Werewolf is a thing of horror – terrorising them and savaging their livestock. But the Doctor recognises it as a lupine wavelength haemovariform – an alien species that requires the specific wavelength of bright moonlight to change forms.

Light Weapon

Just as the alien needed moonlight to transform, the Doctor realised that too much light could kill it. Sir Robert's telescope was built to project a super-intense beam of light powerful enough to destroy both alien parasite and, tragically, its innocent human host.

Unwilling to break through a door smeared with mistletoe, the Werewolf reveals an odd weakness – fear of the parasitic plant.

Gelth

PITY THE GELTH! These formless creatures have been trapped in a gaseous state ever since the Time War, but they long to have physical existence again. An advance party of Gelth make their way to 19th-century Cardiff where they ask a young girl for help. But there are more than three or four Gelth left, there are billions, and they are killers!

Blue eyes turn red once the Gelth are through the Rift

The Rift

The city of Cardiff is the location of a weak point in space and time. Known as the Rift, it is where connections are formed with other eras and places and is the cause of the many ghost stories circulating in the area. Having grown up on the centre of the Rift, servant girl Gwyneth has become part of it. It has given her "the sight" – the ability to read minds.

The Rift is weakest at 7 Temperance Court, home to Sneed and Co. undertakers. Here, the Doctor communicates with the Gelth via psychic Gwyneth. He allows them use of the corpses, just until he can find them a new home.

The Dead Walk

Decomposing human bodies at the funeral parlour produce gas, which forms the perfect home for the gaseous Gelth. They plan to kill the whole human race and use their gas-producing bodies as vessels.

Form changes when Gelth cross the Rift

Gelth Facts

• The Gelth need a gaseous atmosphere to survive – 19th-century gas pipes provide an ideal environment.

• It takes three months of hijacking Sneed's corpses before the Gelth manage to communicate their request to Gwyneth at a seance.

• Without a proper bridge across the Rift, the weakened Gelth are only able to inhabit corpses for short periods of time.

• When the gaseous Gelth animate cadavers, they stimulate the human's dead brain so the corpse becomes aware of details of its former life.

Bridge Between Worlds

When the truth is revealed – that there are billions of Gelth and they plan to take over Earth – Gwyneth, who is their link across the Rift, sacrifices herself by blowing up the room full of gas.

Wings can lift considerable weight

Claws can rip flesh

Krillitanes

WHEN THE DOCTOR first met the Krillitanes, they appeared human, apart from having very long necks. But the next time he encounters them, they have become bat-like. A composite race, the Krillitanes pick the best physical elements from the creatures they conquer and incorporate them to create an improved form.

Jaws ideal for eating children

The Krillitanes have had wings for nearly ten generations, ever since they invaded the planet Bessan, where they made a million widows in one day.

Substitute Teachers

If they crack the Skasas Paradigm – also known as the God Maker and the Universal Theory – the Krillitanes will be able to control time, space and matter. They need the brains and imagination of children, enhanced by Krillitane oil, so they pose as staff at Deffry Vale High School and set the pupils to work.

Bat Beings

The Krillitanes resemble bats in more ways than just their wings. They sleep hanging upside down and have very sensitive hearing. This means that they dislike loud noises.

A simple morphic illusion cloaks the Krillitanes in human form. However, it barely takes a moment to shrug off their disguise, should they need to use their Krillitane abilities.

Krillitane Facts

Prefers human form of head teacher Mr Finch to bat-like body

- When there is no fresh flesh to feed on, the Krillitanes sustain themselves with vacuum-packed rats.
- The Krillitanes are extremely strong and can move very fast.
- The creatures have changed their physiology so often that the oil they use to make the children more intelligent has become toxic to them.
- As well as physical attributes, the Krillitanes steal technology from other races, such as the means to create a deadlock seal.

BROTHER LASSAR

SS *Madame de Pompadour*

THE SS MADAME *de Pompadour* is one of the great energy trawlers of the 51st century. It was originally crewed by humans assisted by clockwork repair robots. However, when the TARDIS arrives onboard, the robots are the only life form left. Rose and Mickey make the grim discovery that, programmed to repair the ship at all costs, the robots used parts of the crew to fix the ship when it was damaged in an ion storm.

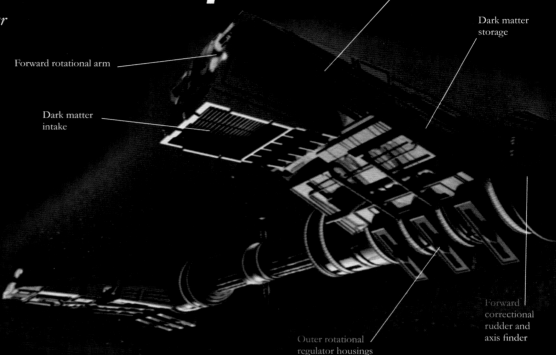

Crew's quarters half way along each arm

Dark matter storage

Forward rotational arm

Dark matter intake

Forward correctional rudder and axis finder

Outer rotational regulator housings

SS Madame de Pompadour Facts

- In the 51st century, humans are dependent on dark matter to fulfil their energy needs. Dark matter is an invisible form of energy that is only identified by its gravitational effects. Rotating arms on the ship scoop up dark matter, which is then stored in the ship's central hub.
- The ship's arms also generate an artificial gravity field, as well as a negative magma field that drives the ship forward.
- The ship boasts antiquated sigmus-style warp engines in case its other power sources fail. The warp engines are powerful enough to punch holes in the universe and create time windows.

To repair the ship's computer, the robots need the brain of Madame de Pompadour, the ship's 18th century namesake. Using their warp drives they punch holes in the universe to create portals to 18th century France. The robots are searching for a window that will lead them to Reinette's 37th birthday, when she will be the same age as the ship.

Spare Part Surgery

With the SS *Madame de Pompadour* suffering severe damage in an ion storm, the robots do what they can to repair it. However, when they run out of mechanical spare parts, the only way to fix the ship is to use living parts of the human crew.

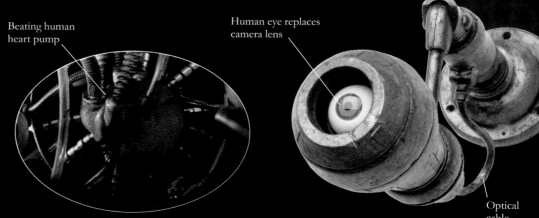

Beating human heart pump

Human eye replaces camera lens

Optical cable

POWER FEED

SECURITY CAMERA

When the repair robots anaesthetise Rose and Mickey and strap them to surgical gurneys, it looks like they, too, will be integrated into the ship's systems.

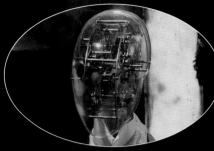

The repair robots are made from 51st century clockwork technology. Old-fashioned and reliable Swiss clockwork techniques are integrated with sophisticated space-age computer chips. The robots are also able to teleport short distances.

Repair Robots

Although their costumes and masks give them the appearance of French courtiers, a loud ticking noise gives them away. Each deadly robot has a sharp blade hidden in its sleeve and can read humans' minds.

The Man in the Fireplace

Using the fireplace portal, the Doctor first meets Reinette as a child and saves her from the clockwork "monster". When he accesses the portal again a few minutes later he is surprised to discover that Reinette is a beautiful young woman.

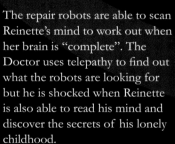

The repair robots are able to scan Reinette's mind to work out when her brain is "complete". The Doctor uses telepathy to find out what the robots are looking for but he is shocked when Reinette is also able to read his mind and discover the secrets of his lonely childhood.

Wig typical of French court

Mask conceals clockwork head

Sharp, retractable blade

Silk stockings cover mechanical legs

REPAIR ROBOT

Madame de Pompadour Facts

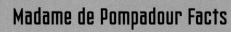

Necklace is a gift from the King

- Born Jeanne-Antoinette Poisson in Paris in 1721, Madame de Pompadour was commonly known as Reinette.
- At a ball in 1745, Reinette caught the eye of the French King and became his official mistress.
- Reinette's title of Madame de Pompadour came from the Paris residence of Pompadour, given to her by the King.

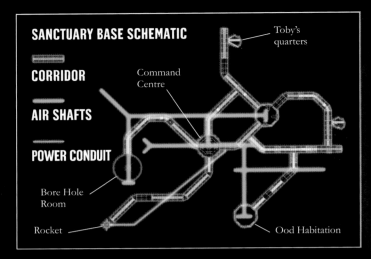

SANCTUARY BASE SCHEMATIC

- CORRIDOR
- AIR SHAFTS
- POWER CONDUIT

Toby's quarters

Command Centre

Bore Hole Room

Rocket

Ood Habitation

Base Floorplan

One of many identical bases used in deep space exploration, Sanctuary Base is constructed from pre-fabricated kits. Separate segments allow the oxygen field to be contained in different parts of the base, and areas can be sealed off in the event of a hull breach. This enables the team to enact "Strategy 9" – sheltering in a locked-down safe area and opening the base's airlocks, sucking invaders into space.

The Beast

WHEN THE TARDIS materialises in a planetary exploration base it is soon clear that all is not quite right. Scripture from a pre-human civilization marks the walls, and the planet is orbiting a black hole – which goes against the laws of physics. The base's crew are drilling to the centre of the planet to harness the mysterious power that keeps it in orbit. But as they mine, an ancient evil trapped in its core begins to stir.

Somehow, the planet is generating enough power to keep it in perpetual geostationary orbit around black hole K37 Gem 5. The Doctor calculates that such a power would need an inverted self-extrapolating reflex of 6 to the power of 6 every 6 seconds – a theoretically impossible figure.

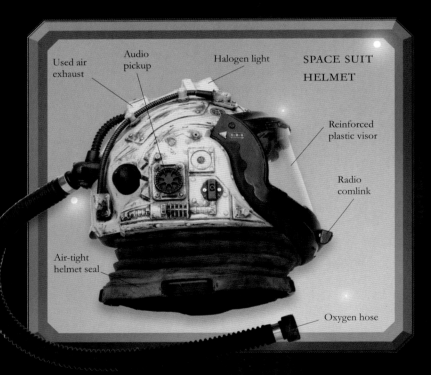

SPACE SUIT HELMET

- Used air exhaust
- Audio pickup
- Halogen light
- Reinforced plastic visor
- Radio comlink
- Air-tight helmet seal
- Oxygen hose

Command Centre

The central desk of the command centre controls all the base's essential functions, including the oxygen field, internal gravity system and rocket link. From here the captain tracks everyone's location from their biochip signals. Overhead shields can be opened to monitor black hole activity.

Surface Work

Protective space suits must be worn on the surface because the planet lacks atmosphere and gravity. At night the drills are shut down by the maintenance trainee, and the base's computer shuts off access to the surface.

Drilling Platform

The planet's solid-rock crust is excavated with robot drills and the base crew painstakingly cut a mineshaft 16 kilometres beneath the surface in a bid to reach the planet's mysterious energy source – an energy giving readings of over 90 Statts on the Blazen scale. The enslaved race, the Ood, do all the dangerous maintenance work on the drilling platform.

Screens monitor the capsule's rate of descent into the mineshaft.

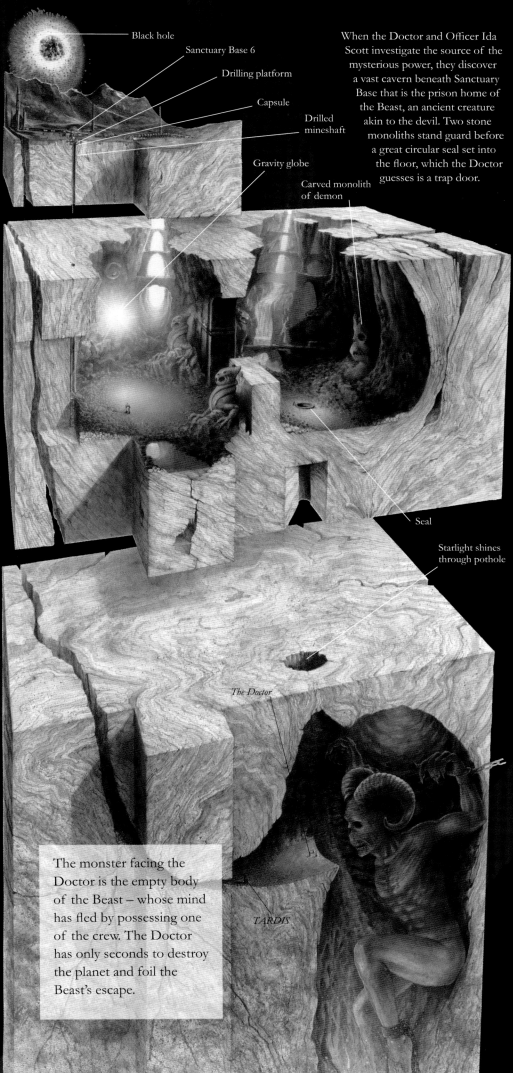

Black hole

Sanctuary Base 6

Drilling platform

Capsule

Drilled mineshaft

Gravity globe

Carved monolith of demon

Seal

Starlight shines through pothole

The Doctor

TARDIS

When the Doctor and Officer Ida Scott investigate the source of the mysterious power, they discover a vast cavern beneath Sanctuary Base that is the prison home of the Beast, an ancient creature akin to the devil. Two stone monoliths stand guard before a great circular seal set into the floor, which the Doctor guesses is a trap door.

The monster facing the Doctor is the empty body of the Beast – whose mind has fled by possessing one of the crew. The Doctor has only seconds to destroy the planet and foil the Beast's escape.

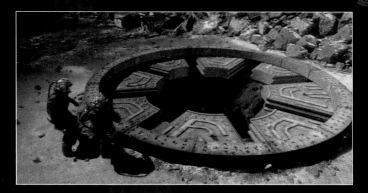

Going Deeper

The Doctor, wearing protective clothing, ponders the strange seal, unable to read the alien writing on it. Sensors indicate that the power source lies beneath. Without warning, the cavern shakes as the trap door's segments slide back to reveal a deep, black chasm. A voice booms from the darkness "The pit is open and I am free!"

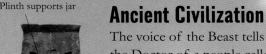

Plinth supports jar

Ancient Civilization

The voice of the Beast tells the Doctor of a people called the Disciples of Light who rose up against him in a time before the universe was created – something the Doctor finds impossible to believe. As if in confirmation of the Devil's words, the Doctor finds cave drawings recording a victory over the Beast and his imprisonment in the pit.

ANCIENT REACTOR

The Perfect Prison

The Doctor realises that the planet is an ingenious prison. If the Beast escapes from the pit, the energy source keeping the planet in orbit will collapse, and the planet will be sucked into the black hole. The air in the pit was supplied by the ancient gaolers so a traveller could stop the Beast's escape by smashing the power source.

Racnoss

THE ARACHNID RACNOSS are born starving and will devour anything, from people to planets. In the Dark Times, near the beginning of the universe, the Fledgeling Empires went to war against the ravenous Racnoss, wiping them out – or so it was thought. One Racnoss Webstar spaceship, hiding from the war, began to attract rocks towards it, creating a planet. Gradually Earth was formed around the ship.

Racnoss Facts

• Each Racnoss can produce miles of strong, thick protein strands that are used to form webs and bind their prey.
• The Racnoss can hibernate without sustenance for billions of years, but when they stir, they are ravenous.
• The Racnoss have mastered teleportation, so do not need to land their webstars on Earth.
• When the Empress refuses the Doctor's offer of a new home, she condemns her entire race to extinction – every Racnoss is wiped out.

Webstar of wonder! The Empress of the Racnoss's ship flies over the Thames on Christmas Eve night, but it is not bringing season's greetings. Bolts of deadly electricity arc from its tips, spreading terror on London's streets. It contains the Racnoss Empress, who has come to rescue the many Racnoss trapped in the Webstar that is at the core of the Earth.

The Empress

The Empress of the Racnoss is on a mission to rescue her children. Long ago, the Time Lords destroyed the Huon energy that forms the source of the Racnoss's power, and the Webstar at the centre of Earth was immobilised. The Racnoss have been sleeping for billions of years when the Empress arrives with a plan to rebuild the Huon particles. She will mix them inside the living test tube of human Donna Noble. The energy will give her access to the ship so she can free her children, who will satisfy their hunger with human flesh!

Tough outer skin is shed when outgrown

"Crown-like" bone structure denotes imperial Racnoss

Pedicle enables free movement of thorax

Blade-like arms slice through prey

Spinnerets at base of abdomen produce web strands

Plasmavores

PLASMAVORES ARE AN alien species who live off the vital life-juices of other creatures. While necessary to their survival, blood-sucking is also an addictive pleasure, and many Plasmavores travel the universe searching for rare species to sample. This mania for blood can lead to psychosis and a severe disregard for the lives of others.

Plasmavore Facts

- The Plasmavore known as Florence Finnegan randomly landed on Earth while on the run from Judoon – galactic hired police. Her crime: murdering the Child Princess of Padrivole Regency Nine on a whim.
- "Florence" quickly identifies the large amounts of blood stored in the Royal Hope Hospital as perfect for "midnight snacks".
- When assimilating blood, Plasmavores generate an exotic plasma energy that attuned individuals like the Doctor can detect. In fact, the Doctor's presence in the hospital can be attributed to him noticing plasma coils surrounding the entire building.

Plasmavore in Hiding

Plasmavores are shape-changers who can assimilate the genetic material of any species whose life juice they drink. One such Plasmavore has taken on the persona of frail 70-year-old Florence Finnegan in order to hide on Earth, in the Royal Hope Hospital. "Florence", wanted for murder, is on the run from intergalactic law enforcers, the Judoon.

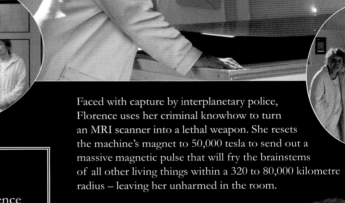

Faced with capture by interplanetary police, Florence uses her criminal knowhow to turn an MRI scanner into a lethal weapon. She resets the machine's magnet to 50,000 tesla to send out a massive magnetic pulse that will fry the brainstems of all other living things within a 320 to 80,000 kilometre radius – leaving her unharmed in the room.

Drone Bodyguards

The Plasmavore calling itself Florence Finnegan is guarded by two Slab henchmen disguised as motorcycle couriers. These basic slave drones are genetically reared for combat and strong-arm work.

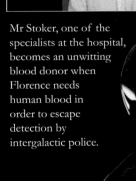

Mr Stoker, one of the specialists at the hospital, becomes an unwitting blood donor when Florence needs human blood in order to escape detection by intergalactic police.

Motorbike gear stolen from blood victims soon after Florence landed on Earth

Motorbike helmet masks Slab's real face

When desperate for blood, Plasmavores will use any ingestion method available at the time. On Earth, the renegade Plasmavore finds a simple bendy straw suitable for its needs.

The Judoon

THROUGHOUT THE UNIVERSE, police authorities come in many shapes, sizes and species. One of the most feared is the private paramilitary security force organised by the thick-skinned, twin-horned species called the Judoon. Each Judoon police officer has the power to administer swift justice: he can arrest, charge, judge, sentence and execute a suspect in a matter of seconds.

Hired Thugs

Judoon police have a reputation of being little more than hired thugs. Their methods are certainly brutal and authoritarian, and carried out without emotion. They focus only on their objective and let nothing stand in the way of justice being done. As they say, "justice is swift". Among other clients, the Judoon enforce laws for the intergalactic regulatory body, the Shadow Proclamation.

Ears with selective hearing

Small eyes betray no emotion

Magnetic seal activates when pressurised helmet is worn

Military fastenings

Language identification scanner

Twin horns for intimidating suspects

Thick skin impervious to most forms of attack

Poor diet contributes to decayed teeth and bad breath

Powerful lungs ensure long-lasting stamina

Voice emitter for use when battle helmet is worn

Bulletproof armour padding

Armoured wrist guard

Variety of weapons and equipment can be atached to utility belt

Battle helmet with breathing equipment

One-way viewing slit

FULL BATTLE ARMOUR

The Judoon's battle armour provides maximum impact protection and functions as a pressurised life-support system for use in toxic environments or on planets with non-breathable atmospheres.

Distinctive boot fastenings – Judoon are said to sleep with their boots on as a sign of their dedication to the job

Thick soles provide protection on uncertain terrain, including toxic spills

In Judoon culture, the studded kilt is a symbol of a warrior

Reinforced knee guard used offensively and defensively in combat

Elaborate military boots

Boots reinforced with bioengineered metal plates to add extra power to bone-shattering kicks

Holster for blaster

Memory chips hold most known languages

LANGUAGE IDENTIFICATION SCANNER

Muzzle guard

Cooling unit

Trigger

JUDOON BLASTER

Blaster gas cartridge chamber

Igniter pin

Grip for Judoon hand

Power cell housing

SPECIES SCANNER

Indelible branding tip

DNA scan emitter

Police Equipment

Judoon police carry high-powered blasters, which they are empowered to fire at their own discretion. A single blast of the deadly energy beam can obliterate a person in a flash. Judoon also carry various scanners that allow them to identify and catalogue suspects by species. Another scanner can sample and assimilate the languages of most known species – ensuring that the Judoon's orders are clearly understood.

Judoon Facts

- The Judoon are organised along military lines, with troops led by commanders.
- The Judoon travel in gigantic tube-shaped spaceships. Originally built as military battle ships, the Judoon chose these intimidating vehicles for their ability to strike fear in others.
- Although the Judoon have no official jurisdiction over Earth, this does not stop them from attempting to capture a plasmavore suspect known to be hiding on the planet. They use an H_2O scoop to suck an entire Earth building onto the surface of the Moon, where they have authority.

The Carrionites

AT THE BEGINNING OF the universe, foul witch-like creatures known as the Carrionites flew the skies of the Rexel Planetary System, using the power of words to manipulate the universe. When the infinitely powerful Eternals discovered the word that would control the Carrionites, they banished them to the Deep Darkness. The Carrionites remained trapped in their prison for millions of years.

Eldest Carrionite

Can transform into beautiful human

Spread "wings" of cloak help witch float in the air

The Grief of a Genius

The Carrionites want to take over the world and they plan to use William Shakespeare to do it. When the famous wordsmith loses his son, his uncontrolled grief and near madness act as a key to the Carrionites' prison. Three escape, and are drawn to Shakespeare on Earth.

The Carrionites act like witches, but they use science not magic. They are planning to create a new empire on Earth, but unlike the numerical equations used in Earth's sciences, the Carrionites use formulae made out of significant shapes and words.

Carrionite Facts

• Carrionites are all female. They try to keep their names secret because a person's name is the most powerful spell of all. However, it can only be used once.

• When a Carrionite forges a connection with a victim's mind, it allows them to sense his or her location and see through his or her eyes.

• Carrionites kill with words, a touch to the heart or the use of poppets. The fumes from their witches' brew can control a man's actions, while his mind is oblivious.

• Until the Carrionites appeared on Earth in 1599, many races – even the Time Lords – thought they were a myth.

The cauldron is used to communicate, to view the past and to brew potions.

A broomstick aids a Carrionite in her flight, although she is able to fly without one.

The Deep Darkness in which the rest of the Carrionites are trapped is shown as a crystal ball.

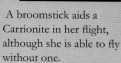

MOTHER DOOMFINGER

Able to materialise instantly by victim's side

Finger can kill with a touch to the heart

Billowing black robes resemble a crow in flight

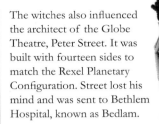

DNA Replication Module

The Carrionites can replicate a person's DNA and control them simply by attaching a lock of hair to a poppet. They use a poppet to make Shakespeare add an extra paragraph to his new play, *Love's Labour's Won*.

The witches also influenced the architect of the Globe Theatre, Peter Street. It was built with fourteen sides to match the Rexel Planetary Configuration. Street lost his mind and was sent to Bethlem Hospital, known as Bedlam.

The doll is made in the shape of the victim

Stabbing the poppet's chest stops the victim's heart

Breaking the poppet in two ensures the victim's death

POPPET

Portal opens, releasing Carrionites into the Globe Theatre

The Hour of Woven Words

When the last lines of *Love's Labour's Won* are spoken, the Globe acts as an energy converter, opening a portal to the Deep Darkness and releasing the Carrionites from their prison. Only Shakespeare – with a little help from Martha – can find the words to close the portal and send the Carrionites back to their eternal prison.

Shakespeare Facts

- William Shakespeare was born in Stratford-upon-Avon in 1564. He started out as an actor, but turned to writing towards the end of the 1580s. He died in 1616 and is now considered the greatest playwright ever.
- Shakespeare married Anne Hathaway and had two daughters, Susanna and Judith, and a son, Hamnet, who died aged 11 in August 1596.
- When Shakespeare closes the portal, all copies of *Love's Labour's Won* are lost with the Carrionites. The world is left to wonder what happened to Shakespeare's mysterious lost play.

The Doctor has met Shakespeare before but the playwright does not recognise him because he has since regenerated.

The Family of Blood

The TARDIS chooses to hide the Doctor in 1913 among the pupils of Farringham School. The boys are being prepared for war, but when the Family comes, they take up arms earlier than expected.

THE FAMILY OF BLOOD ARE HUNTERS with an acute sense of smell, but their life span is only three months. In their natural form they are merely balls of gas, but they are able to take the bodies of other intelligent beings and gain their strength and physical abilities. However, these feeble forms are soon expended, so they want the Doctor's body, which will give one of their number the many lives of a Time Lord.

Family of Mine

The Family's bond is strong and the nameless aliens refer to themselves only in terms of kinship: Father of Mine, Mother of Mine, Son (or Brother) of Mine, Daughter (or Sister) of Mine. Son of Mine is the natural leader and favoured child – he is the one for whom the Family seek immortality.

Body Snatchers

When their hunt for the Doctor brings them to England, each Family member takes on a human shape. The mind of each victim is entirely consumed – memory traces may survive, but not enough to enable the Family to pass as their assumed species without arousing suspicion.

A Vortex Manipulator stolen from a Time Agent allows the Family to track the Doctor. Once on Earth, their spaceship is concealed by an invisibility shield.

Schoolboy Jeremy Baines is fetching illicit beer from Blackdown Woods when he stumbles across the Family. On investigating, his body is taken over by Son of Mine.

Martha suspects something is wrong with maid Jenny when she agrees to share a teapot of gravy. Jenny was snatched by the Family's scarecrow soldiers and has been consumed by Mother of Mine.

The Family Facts
- The Family's strong sense of smell is just as keen within their human bodies.
- Their sense of smell can be fooled by olfactory misdirection, or "ventriloquism of the nose", an elementary trick for the Doctor.
- Family members communicate with each other telepathically. In moments of extreme trauma, they feel each other's pain.
- The laser gun is the Family's weapon of choice. It shoots energy bolts that disintegrate its targets instantly.

The scarecrows, who were turned by the Family into moving soldiers, are sent to locate a body for Father of Mine. They find Farmer Clark in his field at Oakham Farm.

Little Lucy Cartwright is happily walking along with her balloon when the scarecrows take her. Her parents soon realise Daughter of Mine is not their child and so are swiftly killed.

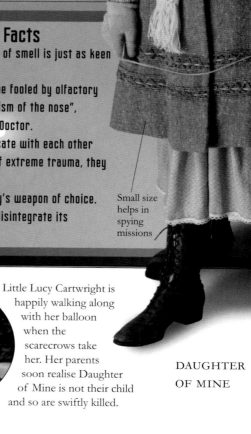

Pupil's body allows access to Farringham school

Gaseous form enters human through eyes

SON OF MINE

MOTHER OF MINE

Small size helps in spying missions

DAUGHTER OF MINE

Childlike appearance disarms foes

Olfactory abilities are concentrated in human nose

FATHER OF MINE

Respectable appearance helps in human society

Scarecrow Soldiers

Scarecrows are not uncommon in rural Herefordshire – but these ones scare more than just crows. Son of Mine creates this scarecrow army. He fashions rough humanoid shapes out of inanimate materials and gives them basic motor and sensory abilities using the process of molecular fringe animation.

"Eyes" allow limited vision

Clothes keep straw in humanoid shape

Following the Family's orders, the scarecrow foot soldiers march inexorably towards the schoolboys' guns. Straw men feel no pain but they are unable to mend themselves if they lose their humanoid form.

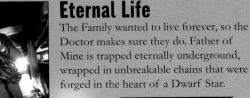

Tim Latimer

Straw filling provides bulk of scarecrow

Return of the Doctor

The Doctor goes to great lengths to make himself human to hide from the Family, not just for his sake, but also to protect them from punishment at his hands. But in the end Martha – helped by psychic schoolboy Tim Latimer – has to bring the Time Lord back before the Family destroy everything.

Shoes provide firm base for straw-filled legs

Quickly masters control of human body

Eternal Life

The Family wanted to live forever, so the Doctor makes sure they do. Father of Mine is trapped eternally underground, wrapped in unbreakable chains that were forged in the heart of a Dwarf Star.

The Doctor tricks Mother of Mine into the event horizon of a collapsing galaxy. She is drawn irresistibly into an inescapable black hole, through which she will fall, screaming, for all eternity.

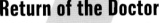

Inside every mirror, occasionally glimpsed but rarely fully seen, is Daughter of Mine. She can never leave her looking-glass prison, where the Doctor visits her once a year.

Son of Mine is suspended in time in a living death, eternally aware but unable to move. The Doctor puts him to work as a scarecrow, guarding the fields of England forever.

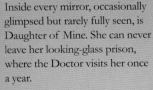

The Master

Has powers
of hypnosis

Respectable
appearance
conceals a
psychopath

THE MASTER WAS one of the Doctor's oldest friends,
but he became his bitterest enemy. They attended the
Time Lord Academy together, but eventually both tired of
Gallifreyan life and became exiles. The Master's evil schemes
were frequently foiled by the Doctor, and he met his final end
when he was sucked into the Eye of Harmony – or so the
Doctor thought.

Hidden in Time and Space

The Master was resurrected by the Time
Lords to fight in the Time War, but he ran
away scared, turning himself into a human
and hiding at the end of the universe.
He was found as a human child on the coast
of the Silver Devastation and eventually
reached the planet Malcassairo where, as
Professor Yana, he tried to help the last
humans find a way to Utopia.

Aged eight, Gallifreyan
children are made to stare
into the Untempered
Schism, a gap in the fabric
of reality. The sight sent
the Master mad, filling
his head forever with the
pounding sound of drums.

Professor Yana's Fob Watch

The Master's Time Lord self is contained
in a fob watch that is identical to the
one the Doctor used when he became
human to escape the Family of Blood.
Martha recognises the watch and brings
it to Yana's attention, overcoming the
perception filter that had kept Yana
from really noticing it.

Weapon of choice was
the Tissue Compression
Eliminator, now it is the
Laser Screwdriver

On opening the fob watch,
the Time Lord's biology,
personality and memory
return. One heart becomes
two, the body temperature
lowers and the respiratory
bypass system is restored.

The Master
has inhabited
at least 17
bodies

You Are Not Alone

Professor Yana opens the fob watch and becomes the Master again, revealing the meaning of the Face of Boe's
message "You are not alone"; the Doctor is not the last of his kind. The restored Time Lord is shot by his
erstwhile assistant, Chantho, but regenerates and escapes to Earth in the Doctor's TARDIS.

LASER SCREWDRIVER

Tip shoots deadly laser beam

Contains technology from Professor Lazarus's Genetic Manipulation Device

Ages a subject when given his or her biological code

Isomorphic controls allow only the Master to use them

The Master's laser screwdriver is similar to the Doctor's sonic screwdriver, but its technology is based on laser beams rather than on focused sound waves.

Worn by the Master on the ring finger of his right hand

SIGNET RING

Rescued from the Master's funeral pyre by an unknown woman

Roedean-educated Lucy Saxon appears to be the Master's devoted wife and companion, but his cruel treatment slowly destroys her, and she is the one who finally shoots him dead.

Elected into Power

After his release from the fob watch, the Master arrives on present-day Earth, where he assumes the identity of "Harold Saxon". He convinces the world that he is a Cambridge graduate and a novelist who became Minister of Defence and rose to prominence after shooting down the alien Racnoss. He is then elected Prime Minister of Great Britain.

The Archangel Network

Harold Saxon launches the Archangel Network. This worldwide mobile-phone network, carried by fifteen satellites, transmits a rhythm that gives the Master hypnotic control over the entire population. But the system backfires on him when Martha uses it to feed power to the Doctor, who is imprisoned by the Master.

Each rocket contains a Black Hole Converter

The entire south coast of England is turned into a rocket shipyard. The rockets are built out of scrap metal by a slave labour force, in preparation for the day that the Master declares war on the universe.

The Master Facts

• The Master has used up his 13 regenerations, but has stolen several bodies to stay alive, including those of Consul Tremas of Traken and an ambulance driver called Bruce.

• As well as "Professor Yana" and "Harold Saxon", the Master's aliases have included Reverend Magister (a country vicar), Professor Thascales (a time-meddling scientist) and Sir Gilles Estram (a thirteenth-century French knight).

• YANA's name – "You Are Not Alone" – is not the only clue left for the Doctor: "Magister" and "Thascales" both translate as "Master", and "Estram" is an anagram.

The Last of the Time Lords

When the Master is defeated, the Doctor will not let him be executed, but he knows that the Master cannot be allowed to go free. As the only other Time Lord in existence, the Master is his responsibility – the Doctor will keep him in the TARDIS and care for him. But Lucy shoots the Master and he refuses to regenerate, preferring death to eternal imprisonment with the Doctor. Despite the Doctor's pleading, the Master dies in his arms, leaving the Doctor as the last of the Time Lords once again.

The distraught Doctor takes the Master's body to a deserted beach, and reverently places it on a funeral pyre.

The Toclafane

WHEN THE HUMAN RACE is faced with the end of the universe in the year 100 trillion, it undergoes its final evolution. The cold, dark nothingness at the end of time drives human beings to regress into the Toclafane – primitive creatures wired into metallic shells. They are rescued by the Master, who transports them from the future to wreak disaster on present-day Earth.

The Master's Secret Weapon

The Master befriends the vulnerable and impressionable Toclafane. Loyal to him without question, they carry out his every destructive instruction. The Master uses them to conquer the Earth and enslave the human race – the first stage in his plan to found a Time Lord Empire across the entire universe.

Merciless killing machines, the Toclafane speed through the air after their victims. They have lasers for long-range attacks and blades for up-close slicing and dicing.

Blades cause extra damage when the sphere rotates

Tough metallic shell can fly through space undamaged

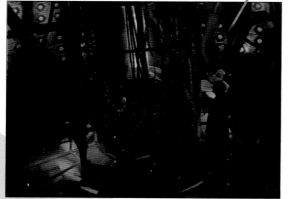

The Toclafane are able to kill their ancestors without wiping out their own existence thanks to the Paradox Machine, a device the Master created by reconfiguring the TARDIS. It forms a temporal paradox that allows the universe to continue, despite the apparent contradiction.

Toclafane Facts

- The Master names the Toclafane after the fictional "Bogeyman" character from a Gallifreyan fairy tale.
- The Toclafane have regressed to primitive human emotions – they enjoy killing without discrimination because "it is fun".
- The childlike Toclafane exhibit the human characteristic of vanity and desire to be "pretty" in their metal shells.
- The Master hopes that it will break the Doctor's two hearts when he discovers that the grotesque Toclafane are the future of humanity.

TOCLAFANE SPHERE

Lasers disintegrate targets

Magnetic clamp holds together the outer shell

Retractable blades and spikes

Wired into each metallic sphere is a withered human head – the last remnant of its human form

All six billion Toclafane share a single collective memory. This holds all the thoughts and experiences of the last humans and is haunted by the never-ending darkness and the terrible cold that human beings faced at the end of time.

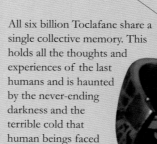

Origin on Malcassairo

In the year 100 trillion, when the universe was coming to an end, the last humans fled the planet of Malcassairo in search of Utopia – a perfect place, believed to have been built by the Science Foundation as part of the Utopia Project to preserve humankind. But Utopia was just a myth and the travellers found nothing but oblivion. Despair led them to evolve into the Toclafane.

CHANTHO

Exoskeleton and mandibles evolved from insects

Highly formulaic speech pattern: every sentence begins "chan" and ends "tho"

Body survives by drinking its own internal milk

Chantho, the last of the insectoid Malmooth race, helped the humans to flee by working on the space shuttle as Professor Yana's devoted assistant.

The spacecraft for the journey used an experimental engine, built using whatever was available to hand, including gluten extract as a binding agent.

Leaving Malcassairo meant escaping the Futurekind, a fierce humanoid race. Some feared that the Futurekind was what humankind would become if they stayed, but their actual fate – the Toclafane – was no better.

World Domination

With the help of the Toclafane, the Master covers the Earth in work camps, churning out rockets for waging war. He is only defeated when the Paradox Machine is destroyed, reversing the invasion and returning the Toclafane to the future.

On the Master's orders, the Toclafane kill one tenth of Earth's population on first contact. Under his regime, they use terror to maintain order among the population.

The Master Race

Sound of the drums beats constantly in head

New supernatural agility and strength

Sense of smell can track the Doctor

Hands ripple with electricity and shoot bolts of energy

ONE MASTER POSES a serious threat to the universe. But six billion of them would be catastrophic. After the Master was shot by his wife Lucy Saxon, the Doctor cradled his body and made sure it was burnt. However, someone stole the Master's ring from the pyre. Through his ring, the Master returns and finds a way to turn every human being into himself. But Earth is just the beginning of his plans.

The Master – Reborn!

An underground cult loyal to the Master performs a ritual to bring him back from the dead. Using his ring, the potions of life, the sacrifice of their own lives and a catalyst, his disciples resurrect his body. The catalyst is his former wife, Lucy Saxon: a tissue with an imprint of her lips, which hold his biometric signature, is added to the elixir.

A New Body

The Master's body may look the same as when he was prime minister Harold Saxon, but it is flawed. Anticipating the Master's return, Lucy had prepared an antidote to the potions of life. She throws it into the mix to sabotage his return. She fails to prevent the Master's resurrection, but does succeed in reducing his body's stability and leaving him with an insatiable hunger.

With new supernatural strength and power, the crazed Master seems unstoppable, but his body is unstable and he's using up his life force.

The Immortality Gate

The Vinvocci race built the Immortality Gate that was found at the foot of Mount Snowdon and commandeered by billionaire Joshua Naismith. The gate is a medical device to cure people by transmitting a template that rebuilds cells. Rather than treating one person at a time, it can cure the populations of whole planets at a time. Driven by the desire to give his daughter immortality, Naismith enlists the Master to fix the machine. However, the Master has his own plans for it.

The Gate runs on nuclear power that is controlled via specialist isolation booths. The feed is manned 24 hours a day and cannot be left unattended: the locking mechanism means that a technician cannot leave one side of the booth until the other side is occupied.

The Naismiths

Joshua Naismith is a ruthless billionaire who will stop at nothing to get what he wants and he possesses his own private army. His daughter Abigail is as vain as he is rich, and both are meddling in alien technology that they do not understand. Joshua is aware of the Master's dangerous reputation, but he arrogantly believes he can control him.

Joshua is the author of the Christmas bestseller *Fighting the Future*

ABIGAIL AND JOSHUA NAISMITH

Cellular Transformation

The Master hijacks Joshua Naismith's plan for the Immortality Gate and uses it to turn everyone on Earth into himself. People are not just genetic copies of the Master, but actually *are* him. All six billion Masters share the same mind. Apart from two people – Donna Noble and her grandfather Wilfred Mott – the human race no longer exists.

Heroic Wilf

Wilf was drawn into the world of the Doctor through his granddaughter Donna, but he too has his own role to play in saving the Earth. He evades transformation because he is in the isolation booth, shielded from the radiation. The old soldier has one more battle left. As the Doctor tracks down the Master, Wilf controls an asteroid rocket, ducking and diving the missiles the Master's armies fire at them.

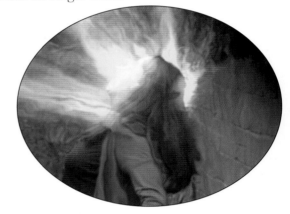

The Doctor's former companion Donna is not affected by the cellular transformation because she is not strictly human. Since her metacrisis, "Doctor Donna" is part Time Lord. However, if she remembers anything about her life with the Doctor, her head will overload and she will die. The Doctor left her with a self-defence mechanism: when her head starts to heat up, she collapses, but remains alive.

Six Billion Masters

As every president, soldier and military leader on Earth, the Master now has all the planet's resources and weapons at his disposal. Six billion crazed warmongers control Earth and plan to turn it into a giant warship to wage war across the universe.

American newscaster Tiffany Wells becomes the Master

Defeat

The Master believes he is now in charge, but he doesn't realise that he is being manipulated. When he finds out that he is merely a pawn in the plans of other Time Lords, he is quick to take his revenge on Rassilon, the Time Lord High Council Lord President.

Time Lords

LONG AGO, THE DOCTOR'S people, the Time Lords, were a great civilisation. They built an advanced society on their planet Gallifrey where they thrived for millions of years. This is how the Doctor chooses to remember them. However, they were corrupted by war and became so dangerous that they posed a threat to time itself.

The Great Time War

After the Daleks discovered that the Time Lords had tried to tamper with history to prevent their creation, they declared war and a massive conflict, the last Great Time War, began. So much fighting twisted the Time Lords' values. Driven to ensure their survival at any cost, they planned the Ultimate Sanction: to destroy the universe and all of time. They would then evolve into a higher consciousness to exist outside of time.

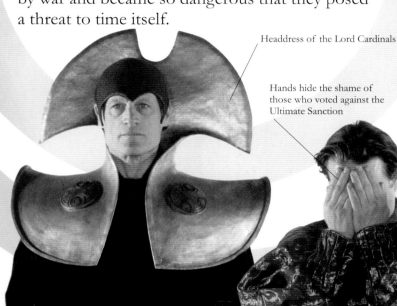

Headdress of the Lord Cardinals

Hands hide the shame of those who voted against the Ultimate Sanction

Rassilon, Lord President of the Council

THE TIME LORD
HIGH COUNCIL

Time Lord High Council Facts

- The High Council is the most senior ruling body of the Time Lords.
- The Council sets Time Lord policy using the knowledge and experience of generations of Time Lords, which is stored in a repository called the Matrix.
- Each chapter of the Time Lords is represented by a Lord Cardinal on the Council.
- The Lord President is the leader of the Council and has virtually absolute power, including life or death over those who disagree with him.

The Visionary assists the Council with predictions of the future.

The Ultimate Sanction

The Great Time War is time-locked, so the events cannot by changed with time travel. On what will be the last day of the war, the trapped High Council are aware of their imminent destruction. They go to the Council to get approval for use of the Ultimate Sanction to escape the time-lock.

Covered eyes are reminiscent of the Weeping Angels

Gallifrey

Gallifrey's Capitol is the seat of Time Lord power. It houses the Academies of Learning, the time-monitoring facilities, the controls for the impenetrable forcefield that protects the planet and the Eye of Harmony – the artificial black hole that provided the energy needed for time travel.

The Time Lords come from Gallifrey, a planet located in the constellation of Kasterborous, some 29,000 light years from Earth. Until its destruction in the Great Time War, Gallifrey is a divided world. The Time Lords dwell in vast citadels enclosed in mighty glass domes, while the Outsiders, the outcasts of Gallifreyan society, lead tribal lives in the wilderness beyond the cities.

Escape to Earth

The Time Lords see Earth as key to their escape. The sound of drums they put in the Master's head is in fact a signal. When every human on Earth becomes the Master, it is amplified by six billion heads. Triangulating all these signals reveals its source – Gallifrey. A whitepoint star diamond is sent to 2010, which the Master uses to return the signal. This creates a physical pathway between Earth and Gallifrey and the Time Lords materialise on Earth and bring Gallifrey into its orbit.

The High Council placed the drumming sound in the Master's head when he was a child. The incessant noise has haunted him for years and driven him mad.

The Doctor's Dilemma

Despite his loneliness, the Doctor is unable to rejoice in the return of his people. He knows he must destroy them all over again. It's a heart-breaking decision, but they are still set on the Ultimate Sanction, which he cannot allow. He shoots the whitepoint star, severing the link and returning the Time Lords to the last days of the Time War.

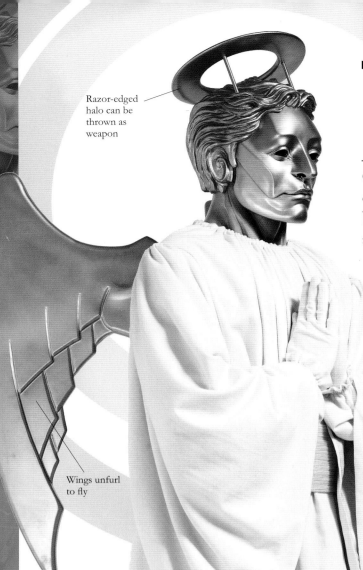

Razor-edged halo can be thrown as weapon

Wings unfurl to fly

Metal hand can deliver karate-style blows

Robot's default position is standing straight, with hands together and head bowed

The Heavenly Host

LIFE BELT

A GROUP OF TOURISTS from the planet Sto in the Cassavalian Belt are on the luxury Max Capricorn Cruiseliner *Titanic*, en route to Earth to experience primitive cultures. On board, they are served by golden robots known as the Heavenly Host, but the angelic-looking creatures are not what they seem.

Sinking the Ship

The *Titanic* is owned by Max Capricorn, who has a secret agenda to destroy the ship, kill the passengers and crew and wipe out life on Earth. Capricorn has even bribed the dying Captain Hardaker to sabotage the ship to cause it to crash.

Dying man has only six months to live

Newly qualified sailor on first trip

Captain Hardaker magnetizes the ship's hull. This attracts meteoroids, which damage the Nuclear Storm Drive engines and cause the *Titanic* to plummet towards Earth. If the ship hits the planet, the nuclear engines will explode and destroy all human life.

Angels of Death

When a Host is asked to fix a passenger's necklace, it nearly breaks her neck! The Host follows orders from Capricorn, and he has programmed them to kill everyone on board the *Titanic*.

Host Facts

- On board ship, the Heavenly Host's job is to provide tourist information and assistance.
- Each Host has the strength of ten men.
- The Hosts' robotics can be temporarily deactivated by an electromagnetic pulse.
- The Doctor initiates Security Protocol One, which overrides any previous instructions and compels a Host to answer three questions.

When the TARDIS crashes into the ship, the Doctor stows away on board. He realises the ship is in danger, but the Host tries to stop him from saving it.

CAPTAIN HARDAKER

MIDSHIPMAN FRAME

The Doctor and the Waitress

Astrid Peth dreams of seeing the stars – and the Doctor makes her dreams come true by taking her to the alien planet Earth. He recognises a kindred spirit in the feisty young waitress and helps her see that nothing is impossible.

ASTRID PETH

Longs to see the universe

Costume based on 1920s waitress

BANNAKAFFALATTA

Red Zocci not to be confused with the green Vinvocci, who have the same distinctive spiky head

MR COPPER

Retired travelling salesman

Spent three years working at spaceport diner

Chest replaced by cybernetics following accident

Has first-class degree in Earthonomics

Head is only remaining organic part

Protective casing contains oxygen field

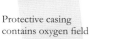

Mechanism produces steam

Titanic's engines can be remote-controlled

Transports passengers between *Titanic* and Earth

TELEPORT BRACELET

London is deserted – except for Wilfred Mott and the Royal Family. The Queen just escapes, as the Doctor pilots the *Titanic* safely over Buckingham Palace.

Vengeful Cyborg

Max Capricorn has vowed revenge on the Board who voted him out of his own company. He believes that he is the victim of anti-cyborg prejudice and hopes that using the *Titanic* to destroy Earth will ruin the company and land his former colleagues in jail for mass murder.

Life-support system constructed in secret on Sto

Max Capricorn Facts

- Max Capricorn Cruiseliners are advertised as "the fastest, the furthest and the best".
- Max ruled his company with a rod of iron for 176 years until he was ousted.
- Max Capricorn names all his cruiseliners himself. He chose *Titanic* after Earth's most famous ship.
- Max has set up offworld accounts and plans to use these secret funds to retire to the beaches of Penhaxico Two.

Astrid falls to her death while trying to save the Doctor. Her molecules are held in stasis and the Doctor sends them to the stars.

Adipose Industries

THE BREEDING PLANET ADIPOSE 3 has been stolen by the Daleks, so the Adipose must find a new way to reproduce. Hired "nanny", Matron Cofelia, needs a planet with high levels of obesity and she finds Earth, where she sets up Adipose Industries. The company's unwitting customers think they are buying a miracle diet product – but really they are forming baby Adipose out of their own flesh!

Observation windows

Hover function enables stationary orbit

NURSERY SHIP

"Seeding" a Level Five planet like Earth – using it to grow another species – is against galactic law. While the Nursery Ship collects the newborn Adipose, the Adiposian First Family murders Matron Cofelia to cover its tracks.

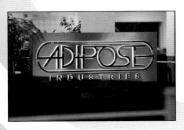

One million customers in Greater London sign up to the Adipose Industries special offer: £45 for three weeks' supply of pills, plus a free gift of an 18-carat gold pendant.

Miss Foster

Matron Cofelia of the Five-Straighten Classabindi Nursery Fleet adopts the alias Foster when she is employed by the Adiposian First Family to facilitate the birth of a new generation of Adipose. Her devotion to her charges is matched only by her callousness towards the humans she utilises in her plans.

Has access to high-level technology

The Adipose

The baby Adipose may appear friendly and sweet as they wave goodbye to Miss Foster, but some of them have already killed, albeit unwittingly. In a crisis, Adipose are programmed to consume their entire human host rather than just fat.

Parthenogenesis changes people's fat into baby Adipose

PENDANT

Pendant attracts fat, binds it together and galvanises it to form a body

Capsule bio-tunes itself to its owner so only affects that person

FAT-EATING PILL

Watch doubles as communicator between Miss Foster and her minions

WATCH

SONIC PEN

Miss Foster's pen has similar properties to the Doctor's sonic screwdriver

Adipose Facts

- Each Adipose consists of exactly one kilogram of living fat.
- In a crisis, Adipose can form themselves from body parts other than fat, but converting bone, hair and internal organs makes them sick.
- Newborn Adipose are small enough to fit through cat flaps.

Adipose are created at 1.10am every morning

The Adipose Industries building is converted into a Levitation Post, ready to float ten thousand baby Adipose up to the Nursery Ship.

Will kill to achieve her goals

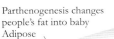

Vespiform

Although prized as a priceless gem, the Firestar is actually a Vespiform Telepathic Recorder. It is psychically connected to the Vespiform and holds the secret of the key to his true identity.

T HERE ARE MANY shape-changing insectivorous life forms in the universe, but none is native to the galactic vector containing Earth. But in 1885, a member of one of these amorphous races – a Vespiform – arrives in India from its hive in the Silfrax galaxy, and takes on a human form to learn about the human race.

Susceptible to insecticides such as piperine, found in pepper

Vespiform is able to fly

Eight feet in length

Morphic residue is left behind when Vespiform transforms from human form

VESPIFORM

An Insect Romance

A purple shooting star heralds the arrival of the Vespiform in Delhi. As "Christopher", he meets Lady Clemency Eddison. She conceives his child, but he is drowned when the River Jumna bursts its banks in the great monsoon, leaving Clemency heartbroken.

Eddison Hall and its estate are passed down the female line, along with the Eddison title.

Anger breaks the genetic lock that prevented the half-human, half-Vespiform child from accessing his true identity.

Loss of stinger renders Vespiform temporarily defenceless

Stinger can be regrown

STINGER

Full of deadly poison

REVEREND GOLIGHTLY

Spends 40 years unaware of his Vespiform heritage

Firestar was a gift from Christopher

Reverend Golightly

In 1926, the Firestar beams the true identity of the Reverend into his mind. He discovers he is the half-Vespiform child given up for adoption. Like the insect he resembles, he attacks humans without compunction, but at the end, he lets Agatha Christie go.

The Doctor poses as Chief Inspector Smith of Scotland Yard to solve the mystery of the murdering insect. Justice of a sort is served when the Vespiform drowns in the lake.

LADY EDDISON

Agatha Christie Facts

- Agatha Christie was born in England on 15th September 1890 and became the "Queen of Crime", the world's best known mystery writer.
- By 1926, she had written only six books, but she went on to pen another sixty mystery novels as well as romances, plays and over 150 short stories.
- Agatha Christie's most famous sleuths are the Belgian detective Hercule Poirot and the shrewd elderly spinster Miss Jane Marple from the village of St. Mary Mead.
- In 1926, Agatha disappeared for eleven days and never explained what happened. Doctors diagnosed amnesia, but some thought it was a publicity stunt or revenge on her cheating husband.

Fiery breath can incinerate humans

Cold water shatters hot stone

Internal magma holds body together

Stone carapace, the dorsal part of the exoskeleton

Pyrovile dust is contained in the vapours from Vesuvius's hot springs, which are breathed in by the mystics of Pompeii to aid their visions.

Pyroviles

EARTH FEELS THE HEAT as the Pyroviles wake up! The fire-loving stone creatures shattered when their escape pod landed on Earth and they lay dormant for thousands of years under Mount Vesuvius, a volcano near the city of Pompeii. But in 62AD, an earthquake heralds their awakening. With much of their technology still intact, the Pyroviles plan to return to their planet, Pyrovillia. But it has been stolen by the Daleks so they must find a new home.

Reconstitution

With their bodies smashed into dust, the Pyroviles need a new form. Inhaled as tiny particles by the citizens of Pompeii, they then force themselves inside the brain, where they use latent psychic talent to bond with their host's body, gradually transforming it into stone.

The magma creatures travel from the heart of Vesuvius to Pompeii via the underground network of hot springs.

Burning Earth

Inside Vesuvius, the Pyroviles blaze with ideas. Their energy converter will harness the power of the lava in the volcano to create a fusion matrix and speed up the conversion of humans into Pyroviles. In their new Empire, the Earth will burn and the oceans will boil.

Vesuvius Facts

- On 23rd August 79AD, Mount Vesuvius erupted with the force of twenty-four nuclear bombs.
- The eruption lasted over twenty-four hours. Many were killed by hot gas and rocks.
- The Romans believed eruptions were caused by giants who had been buried under mountains by the gods.
- Like typical Romans, Caecilius the marble dealer and his family who meet the Doctor, regularly gave thanks to the household gods to avoid bad fortune.

Pompeii was a popular holiday destination for Romans. It's unknown exactly how many of the town's 20,000 inhabitants died, but the scale of the disaster in 79AD was unprecedented.

Sibylline Facts

- The name "Sibyl" was given to women who were thought to be possessed by the god Apollo.
- The Sibyl were believed to have the power of prophecy.
- Joining the Sibylline Sisterhood was a life-long commitment and was considered a prestigious and honourable occupation for Roman women.
- The Sibylline books were a collection of oracles that were consulted when Rome was in trouble.

Voice of the Pyrovile speaks through her

Entire body has become stone

HIGH PRIESTESS

The High Priestess of the Sibylline shows her heart of stone when she tries to kill the Doctor. She is halfway between human and Pyrovile, but thinks that her painful transformation is a blessing from the gods.

The painted eyes are a symbol of the Sibylline.

False Prophet

Thanks to her knowledge of history, Donna knows that Pompeii will be destroyed, but the Sibylline Sisterhood disagree. Scared and angry at this dissenting voice, the seers decree that she must pay for her words with death.

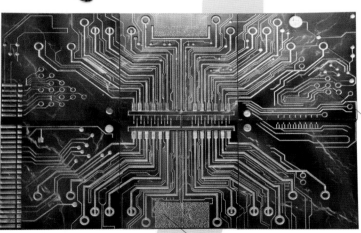

ENERGY CONVERTER

Design came to Lucius Dextrus in a dream – from the Pyroviles

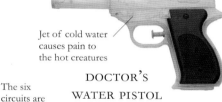

Jet of cold water causes pain to the hot creatures

DOCTOR'S WATER PISTOL

The six circuits are carved from marble

Pyrovillian Prophecy

Vesuvius's eruption is so powerful that it cracks open a rift in time. Ripples from the explosion radiate back to the start of the Pyrovillian timeline – the earthquake in 62AD. This disruption of time gives the Pyrovile-infected citizens like Lucius Petrus Dextrus the ability to see echoes of the future.

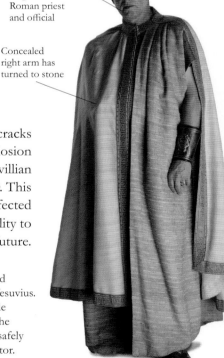

Pompeii's Chief Augur – a Roman priest and official

Concealed right arm has turned to stone

LUCIUS PETRUS DEXTRUS

Not even the Pyroviles' escape pod would survive the eruption of Vesuvius. But as it is programmed to evade danger, it removes itself from the heart of the volcano and lands safely nearby with Donna and the Doctor.

The Doctor's Dilemma

Pompeii or the world? The Doctor has to choose. Vesuvius's lava will be used up in the Pyroviles' plan, but by stopping the aliens, the eruption goes ahead and the whole of Pompeii is destroyed.

Saving the Caecilius Family

History states that those who stayed in Pompeii died and the Doctor cannot change that. But history does not list every individual, so Donna encourages the Doctor to look beyond the letter of the law. He can save one family and he saves the Caeciliuses, which could have been what always happened.

Sontaran

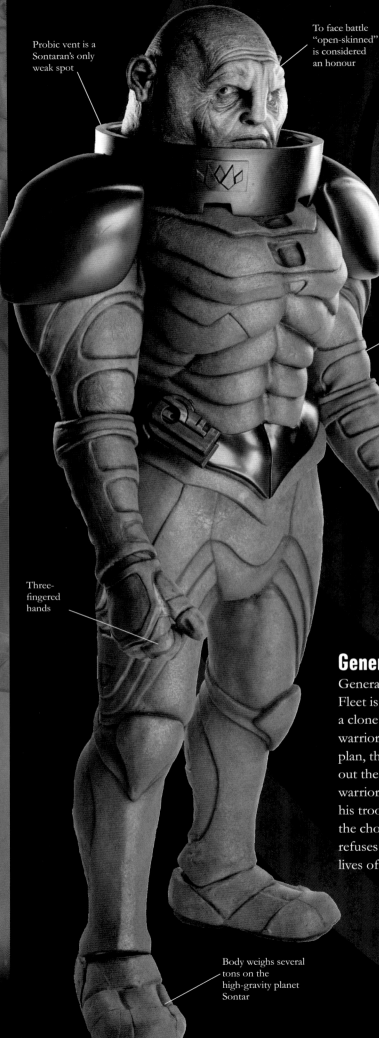

Probic vent is a Sontaran's only weak spot

To face battle "open-skinned" is considered an honour

Muscles designed for load-bearing, rather than leverage

Three-fingered hands

Body weighs several tons on the high-gravity planet Sontar

S ONTARANS CARE ABOUT NOTHING but war. They have been fighting their deadly enemy, the Rutans, for 50,000 years, and there is no end in sight. Their every action serves to further their cause, whether it is searching for a strategically advantageous position or increasing the number of Sontaran warriors to take part in the conflict. Combat is glorious for Sontarans and to die heroically in battle is their ultimate goal.

Attack of the Clones

All Sontarans look similar – because they are clones. At their military academy on Sontar, one million battle-hungry Sontaran clones are hatched at every muster parade. Under the charge of Sontaran High Command, each warrior is immediately given a rank and dispatched on a battle mission.

General Staal, the Undefeated

General Staal of the Tenth Sontaran Battle Fleet is charged with turning Earth into a clone world to create more Sontaran warriors. When the Doctor disrupts this plan, the vengeful Staal prepares to wipe out the human race. As a good Sontaran warrior, he is proud to enter the fray with his troops, and when the Doctor gives him the choice between death or defeat, he refuses to submit, even though it costs the lives of himself and all his soldiers.

Staal enlists the help of scientist Luke Rattigan and his students to lay the foundations of a clone world on Earth. But he has nothing but contempt for these human helpers and proposes to use them for target practice when their usefulness is at an end.

Fires a disabling beam that can temporarily render a person useless

Emits an energy pulse that can repair systems like the teleport

SWAGGER STICK

Sontaran Spacecraft

The Tenth Sontaran Battle Fleet consists of a Command Ship and a number of capsules that can be moved into position when Battle Status is enjoined. Sontaran ships are impervious to nuclear missiles.

Spherical capsules detach from main ship

COMMAND SHIP

Sphere spins through space

Small enough to avoid detection by radar

Piloted by individual Sontaran

SCOUTSHIP

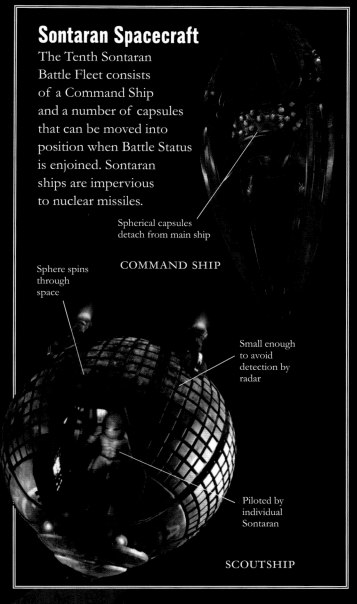

Laser beams kill instantly

Display indicates power usage

Designed for three-fingered grip

SONTARAN GUN

Clips onto hand-held blaster to make it a rifle blaster

Attaches to Sontaran's belt

Wrist-comms units enable communication between the Command Ship War Room and Sontaran forces on Earth.

CLIP-ON BLASTER EXTENSION

Commander Skorr, the Bloodbringer

Second-in-command Skorr leads the Attack Squad to Earth, relieved to finally be facing combat. He welcomes his death in battle at the hands of UNIT's Colonel Mace, and his only regret is that he will not see the ultimate victory of the Sontarans.

ATMOS DEVICE

All ATMOS cars are fitted with this Sontaran-controlled satellite navigation system.

ATMOS Industries

The Atmospheric Omission System (ATMOS) is a driver's dream: as well as being a satnav system, it reduces carbon emissions to zero using an ionising nano-membrane carbon dioxide converter. But its true purpose is to release a killer gas that will change Earth's atmosphere into food for Sontaran clones.

Luke Rattigan

Teen genius Luke Rattigan is tired of being laughed at on Earth, so he is quick to create ATMOS for the Sontarans, mistakenly believing that his reward will be a planet populated solely by clever people.

The teleport between the Command Ship and Luke's Academy is the Sontarans' undoing – through it betrayed Luke is able to wreak revenge.

Bony ridge protects the facial area

Nutrients need to be replenished frequently

Gills "breathe" liquid nutrients on land

Overalls designed for manual work

Pockets carry ammunition

Protective kneepads

Boots enable sure and silent movement

HATH GABLE

The Hath

BY THE 61ST CENTURY, Earth's resources are dwindling and its population is increasing, so humankind must look for other planets to colonise. The fish-like Hath assist humans in their search and eventually the allies discover a suitable planet named Messaline. However, the death of the mission commander triggers a generations-long war between humans and the Hath.

Messaline

The three moons of Messaline reveal a barren wilderness of bleak moors and treacherous bogs. The high levels of ozone and radiation make the planet's surface uninhabitable, so the visitors must build their colony underground.

Warrior Hath

The Hath are intelligent, emotional humanoid creatures capable of great loyalty to those who earn it. However, conflict breaks out easily between the Hath and other species due to their fearsome tempers, a trait that also makes them formidable opponents in battle.

The Hath and humans become bitter enemies in the search for "the Source", which they both believe to be the breath of their creator.

Hath Facts

- Although Hath speech is difficult to decipher due to the bubbling of their nutrient flasks, humans and Hath are able to communicate.
- The Hath have a similar skeletal structure to humans, including ball-and-socket joints in their shoulders.
- Hath are experts in genetics and have a high level of technological knowledge.
- Natural pioneers, the Hath made their own way into space before teaming up with humans who could help further their quest by sharing technology and resources.

The Hath have piscine genes in their ancestry, but technology allows them to live on land. Flasks of the nutrient liquid that they breathe operate similarly to a human's underwater oxygen tank.

War

After the death of mission commander General Cobb, the humans and the Hath quarrel over who should assume control of the operation and the colonists divide into rival factions. Progenation machines are reprogrammed to create soldiers, embedding military history and tactics in the generations that spring from them.

General Cobb commands the human army

GENERAL COBB

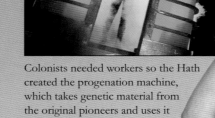

Colonists needed workers so the Hath created the progenation machine, which takes genetic material from the original pioneers and uses it to form fully grown beings of the same race.

Two hearts, like a Time Lord

Sets off explosives with short delay, originally designed for building work but now used as a weapon

DETONATOR

The Doctor's Daughter

When the TARDIS lands on Messaline, a soldier forces the Doctor's hand into a progenation machine. A tissue sample is extrapolated and accelerated, and within minutes the Doctor becomes a father! The blonde teenager is genetically a Time Lord, but has been engineered to be a soldier.

Soldiers are not assigned names, so Donna calls the Doctor's daughter "Jenny" because she is a "genetic anomaly".

Ability to regenerate

Jenny

Despite their physiological likeness, the Doctor claims there is no real relationship between them. However, he grows to care for his "daughter" and Jenny learns compassion and wanderlust from her "father". When she is shot, her Time Lord DNA enables her to survive.

An expert in unarmed combat

Super-temp Donna realises the mystery numbers on the walls are the building completion dates. This means that, despite having been on Messaline for "generations", the colonists have actually only been there for seven days!

Doctor Jones

A doctor treats anyone, and when you are a space-traveller, that includes aliens. Martha resets Peck's dislocated shoulder and gains the trust of the injured Hath and his colleagues. In return, Peck insists on accompanying her across the perilous surface of Messaline, and ends up rescuing Martha from a deadly swamp.

Weapon of Hath design

Ammunition magazine

HATH PECK

The Source

Tales of the Source have been passed down through generations of colonists. It turns out to be a terraforming machine – a device to make bare planets habitable. The gases it releases into the atmosphere accelerate evolution on Messaline, rejuvenating the ecosystem and creating abundant plant life.

Vashta Nerada

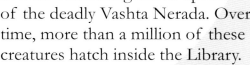

By the 51st century, there are many ways to experience narratives – holovids, direct-to-brain downloads, fiction mist – but people still love books! The Felman Lux Corporation creates a vast planet-sized Library controlled by the immensely powerful computer called CAL. However, the corporation doesn't realise that the newly printed books have been made from trees containing micro-spores of the deadly Vashta Nerada. Over time, more than a million of these creatures hatch inside the Library.

A swarm of Vashta Nerada animates the space suit and uses neural relay to communicate

"4022 Saved"

One hundred years before the Doctor arrives, the Vashta Nerada enter their deadly hatching cycle. There are 4022 humans in the Library at the time, and nowhere is safe for them to be teleported to, so CAL saves them all to her hard drive.

Vashta Nerada Facts

- Their name means "the shadows that melt the flesh" because they strip their victims to the bone in seconds. They are also known as "piranhas of the air".
- The Vashta Nerada are found on a billion worlds, including Earth, where they live mainly on roadkill.
- The creatures hunt by latching on to a living food source and keeping it fresh until they devour it.
- They normally live in the darkness, but can also be seen as the dust in sunbeams.

The man-eating swarms create an extra shadow

Silence in the Library

When the human-hunting Vashta Nerada hatch in the Library, it seals itself, leaving a single message: 'the lights are going out'. The Library's creator, Felman Lux, cannot decode the seals and enter, but he exhorts his descendants to keep trying and to safeguard CAL.

A group of expeditioners led by River Song venture into the Library, but many fall prey to the Vashta Nerada. The swarms devour human flesh, then animate the remaining skeleton.

CHARLOTTE ABIGAIL LUX

The Library computer is known by her initials, CAL.

Charlotte watches the Library through living cameras

SECURITY CAMERA

The Negotiator

The Doctor brokers a deal with the Vashta Nerada: he will allow them free reign over the Library for eternity, but in exchange they must give him a day's grace to evacuate everyone trapped on CAL. He plans to sacrifice himself to stabilize the power to CAL, but River Song insists on taking his place.

Book-loving Charlotte Abigail Lux was terminally ill, but her father, Felman Lux, wouldn't let her die. Instead, her mind became the main command node of the Library, which Lux built for her eternal pleasure.

The Flood

HUMANITY'S EXPLORATION of the stars makes a leap forward in the year 2058 with the first human settlement on Mars. Bowie Base One is established to study the planet to see if a colony is viable. The pioneering crew tap into an underground glacier in the Gusev Crater for water supplies, unaware that the water holds a viral life form known as the Flood. A faulty filtration system leads to some of the crew becoming possessed.

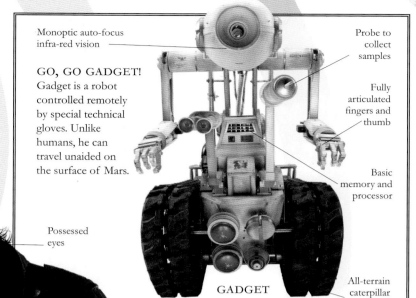

GO, GO GADGET! Gadget is a robot controlled remotely by special technical gloves. Unlike humans, he can travel unaided on the surface of Mars.

Monoptic auto-focus infra-red vision

Probe to collect samples

Fully articulated fingers and thumb

Basic memory and processor

Possessed eyes

All-terrain caterpillar tracks

GADGET

Adelaide wanted to travel into space ever since she saw a Dalek as a child

Tough Talking

Strong-minded Captain Adelaide Brooke leads the team on Bowie Base One. Thanks to her intellect and determination, she was the first non-American NASA candidate, the first woman on Mars, and is famous for her research. The Doctor greatly admires Adelaide, calling her the "woman with starlight in her soul".

The Flood Facts

- The Flood virus infects a victim through contaminated water. It possesses and transforms a person's body and mind, leaving no trace of their personality.
- Infected people are able to gush an endless supply of water from their mouths and hands.
- The possessed can survive on the surface of Mars without protective suits or oxygen.
- Host bodies are driven to perpetuate the Flood by infecting more people and hunting out new sources of water.

Water drips constantly from the body

Watery Nightmare

Six of the nine crew on Bowie Base One fall victim to the Flood virus and have their bodies transformed: their mouths crack, their teeth blacken, and their eyes turn a haunting light-blue. Controlled by a hive mind, the zombie-like creatures try to infect the rest of the crew and use them to reach water-rich Earth.

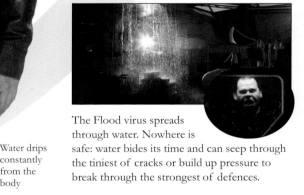

The Flood virus spreads through water. Nowhere is safe: water bides its time and can seep through the tiniest of cracks or build up pressure to break through the strongest of defences.

Self-destruct

When Adelaide realises the crew is doomed, she arms the base's nuclear self-destruct to stop the Flood reaching Earth. Those infected perish in the explosion, but the Doctor steps in to rescue the remaining healthy crew in the TARDIS.

LADY CHRISTINA
DE SOUZA

Elegant and poised
aristocrat

San Helios

HALFWAY ACROSS the universe in the Scorpion nebula, the civilisation of San Helios has been wiped out by scavenging stingrays who devour everything in their path. And their next stop is planet Earth! All that stands in their way is a handful of passengers on the number 200 bus that has fallen through a wormhole. But they are no ordinary passengers – one of them is the Doctor and he'll do everything to get them all home.

Lady Christina de Souza

Bored with her life of privilege, Lady Christina has turned her back on her upbringing and become a notorious jewel thief. She is being chased by the police when she leaps on the number 200 bus. She steals for the adventure – of which she has plenty with the Doctor when they end up on San Helios.

Tight-fitting clothes
for nimble
acrobatics

Belonged to King
Athelstan over 1000
years ago

Gold cup is
sacrificed
to weld together a
contraption to get
the bus home

CUP OF ATHELSTAN

Christina uses her wits as an audacious thief. In it for the thrills, she swipes the Cup of Athelstan from right under the noses of four museum security guards.

Sturdy and silent
rubberised boots

The Mighty 200

One minute the number 200 bus is entering a tunnel in London traffic. The next it is battered and stranded on the sandy world of San Helios. It fell through a wormhole, but returning to Earth is not so simple: the driver tries to walk through and is fried to a skeleton.

Sand is clogging the engine, the wheels are stuck and the bus is out of petrol. The Doctor calms the panicking passengers and makes them see that they must all work together.

The bus takes the brunt of
the wormhole, protecting
the passengers inside like a
Faraday Cage

Sand is all that's left of
San Helios. The Stingrays
have turned the planet
barren in less than a year

Unbeatable global call tariffs

Ravenous Stingrays

These scavenging stingrays swarm in their billions and travel from world to world consuming everything in their path. When a planet is stripped bare, they fly in a massive formation, circling at high speed until they rupture space and create a wormhole. Then they pass through to another unsuspecting world and repeat the cycle.

Metal is eaten and passed through into bones

Compound eyes just like flies

Communicate via clicking noises and moving mandibles

Teeth capable of eating through anything

Body is size of a small car

The Doctor sees a sandstorm on the horizon but soon realises it is a swarm of stingrays. If they reach the wormhole they created, Earth will be history.

Feed off organic waste

Telepathic translator

Metal exoskeleton can pass through wormhole undamaged

Tail steers when flying

Malcolm is ecstatic to speak to his hero the Doctor

Tritovores

Two Tritovores — a race of humanoid flies — are also stranded on San Helios. They capture the Doctor and Christina, believing that their bus is a weapon that caused their ship to crash. However, they soon realise the swarm of Stingrays is responsible and they join forces, but before they can reach the bus, the Tritovores fall prey to a stingray.

Scientific Advisor

The Doctor calls UNIT on a souped-up mobile and makes a new best friend of genius Malcolm Taylor who writes a program to seal the wormhole against the stingrays. Even under orders, Malcolm refuses to close it until all the passengers are safe.

Impulse laser pistol

The Doctor is impressed by the Tritovores' technology and is glad to find anti-gravity clamps, which, attached to the wheels of the bus, help the bus fly home.

Once the threat of the Swarm has ended, the Doctor is eager to move on. Even though they make a great team, he won't let Lady Christina travel with him. He has lost every companion he has travelled with and is not willing to let that happen again.

DOCTOR MALCOLM TAYLOR

Prisoner Zero

Prisoner Zero Facts

- Prisoner Zero is an inter-dimensional multi-form, meaning it can change its shape and even copy the identities of more than one creature at a time.
- The first time Prisoner Zero duplicates someone with whom it has formed a psychic link, they fall into a deep coma. They stay unconscious until the link is broken.
- Prisoner Zero can create perception filters to stop it being seen. It can also use them to conceal anything it chooses, which is how Prisoner Zero hides in a room in Amy's house for 12 years.
- Multi-forms can live for millennia.

Prisoner Zero is extremely dangerous. Amy narrowly escapes death when she discovers it in her house.

A HIGHLY DANGEROUS creature, known as Prisoner Zero, has escaped from an alien race called the Atraxi. A crack in space allows the fugitive to flee to Earth where it hides in the house of a young girl named Amelia Pond. The creature remains concealed there for twelve years using its shape-shifting abilities to avoid detection. But it's only a matter of time before the Atraxi locate it – with grave consequences for Earth.

Shape-shifter's natural form

Malevolent yellow eyes have vertical slit pupils

Gelatinous, snake-like body

Internal organs glow below the translucent skin

Mouth has razor-sharp teeth and a ridged tongue

Warning from the Wall

For too long, young Amelia Pond has been worried about the crack in her bedroom wall and the voice saying, "Prisoner Zero has escaped" that comes from it. When the Doctor arrives, he uncovers the Atraxi prison guard behind the crack who warns him that Prisoner Zero is hiding on Earth.

Easy Targets

To adopt another form, Prisoner Zero must first create a psychic link with a living creature. Before it can copy an appearance, the victim must be in a dormant state. Coma patients in Leadworth Hospital provide Prisoner Zero with numerous different guises. It's only a nurse called Rory Williams who suspects something is amiss when he sees the comatose patients out and about in Leadworth.

Prisoner Zero's psychic link with its victims enables it to take the form of anything the victim dreams about, like their dogs or children.

The Atraxi

The Atraxi are a sophisticated race of aliens who use advanced technology to search for Prisoner Zero on Earth. They scan the entire planet to detect alien life but miss their escapee because it has taken human form. The

fugitive is so dangerous that the Atraxi are willing to destroy Earth to stop it escaping. They break Article 57 of the Shadow Proclamation when they surround Earth, seal off its atmosphere and threaten to boil the planet if Prisoner Zero does not surrender.

Prisoner Zero copies a coma patient dreaming of her two daughters

When threatened, the Atraxi bares its teeth, giving away its true identity

Ships contain enough firepower to incinerate Earth

Crystalline structure is similar to a snowflake.

ATRAXI SHIP

Voice Swap

Amy and Rory are shocked to see that Prisoner Zero has attacked Leadworth Hospital. Cautiously approaching the coma ward, they find a terrified mother and her two daughters, but Amy soon realises they are actually Prisoner Zero when the shape-shifter confuses their voices and one of the girls speaks with the mother's voice.

Lurking in her house, Prisoner Zero has watched Amy grow up and seen how she waited 12 years for the Doctor. It uses the bond between them to impersonate them both

THE ZERO VIRUS

The Doctor tries to alert the Atraxi by using his sonic screwdriver but it breaks before they detect it so he must find another way to get their attention. Using Rory's phone, he creates a computer virus to reset every counter on Earth to zero.

As the computer virus takes hold all clocks and counters around the world turn to zero

With the help of Earth's space and alien experts, the Doctor's reset virus spreads across the world. The Atraxi trace the phone to find the Doctor and Prisoner Zero's location.

Duplicate Doctor

The Doctor transmits photos of the coma patients to the Atraxi to identify Prisoner Zero but it now has a psychic link to Amy. She dreams of herself as a child with the Doctor, so Prisoner Zero impersonates them both. The real Doctor gets her to dream of Prisoner Zero's true form. It is then easily identified by the Atraxi and recaptured, saving Earth.

Smilers

Demonic red eyes strike fear into the heart of anyone who looks into them

Head rotates to show three different faces: smiling, frowning and angry

Long purple robe hides a mechanical body

Mandy is the girl who explains to the Doctor and Amy about the Smilers and life on Starship UK

IN CLASSROOMS, in the elevators, in the streets — the android Smilers are everywhere on the Starship UK. As the monumental ship travels between the stars in the 33rd century, Smilers keep watch over the British population, letting them know what is good and what is bad. Any lawbreakers discover that the smiling law enforcers have a very nasty side to them!

Watching over you

The British people live in fear of the Smilers. The Doctor spots that no one walks near their booths, and while the Starship is battered, untidy and filthy, the Smilers' booths are spotless. It's another clue that there is something not quite right about life on board the ship.

On board the Starship UK, people travel by Vators. These are vast elevators operated by Smilers that travel through district blocks.

Smiler Facts

- Smilers are an extension of the ship's security system. They observe life and activity on Starship UK and maintain order.
- There have been Smilers mounted in booths on the Starship UK since it left Earth in the 29th century.
- The androids are self-repairing and if damaged can return to full working order in minutes.
- The front of the Smilers' booths can open so they can leave and deal with law-breakers.
- Everyone on board the Starship UK is terrified of the Smilers. They don't go near them if they can help it.
- The Smilers' booths are kept clean by the frightened citizens of the Starship UK.

If citizens obey the rules, the Smiler's face is happy and placid

Plaque on the booth says "Smiler"

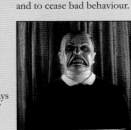

A frowning face is a warning that laws are being broken, and to cease bad behaviour.

This expression is a final warning before punishment is meted out.

Liz Ten

Liz Ten is Queen Elizabeth the Tenth and ruler of Starship UK. She suspects that her government is keeping secrets from her and tries to find out what's going on. She doesn't realise that every ten years she discovers the terrible secret but each time she chooses to forget it.

Liz Ten is about 300 years old

Porcelain mask allows Liz to walk inconspicuously among her subjects

Sumptuous red velvet cape is a clue to Liz's regal identity

Winders

The Winders are the police force of Starship UK. They wind up the Smilers and are the only people to know the terrible truth about the Starship UK — that it's not a working spaceship at all but a ship built upon a suffering Star Whale. They have taken an oath to keep this secret and uphold the system that stops people asking questions.

The Winders are so devoted to serving the Starship UK system they have become cyborgs — part human, part Smiler.

The Winders wear long dark robes with hoods that conceal their "Smiler" side until they choose to reveal it.

Ring contains knock-out gas

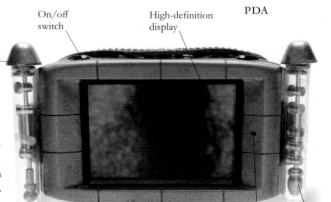

WINDER

WIND-UP KEY BOX

Key

Wind-up key

When wound up with the key the mainspring provides power

On Starship UK many things such as the street lamps are wind-up operated. The Winders patrol the streets and have keys for all of them.

Sighting

Gun barrel

Energy blast converter

Energy focus

Isomorphic trigger

LIZ TEN'S GUN

Battery power

Liz Ten's gun fires energy blasts that can stop the formidable Smilers but only temporarily because they are able to repair themselves.

LIZ TEN'S PDA

On/off switch

High-definition display

Eternal momentum battery

Liz Ten communicates with her government officials through her PDA. The high-tech device can also be used to track people. Liz gives her PDA to the Doctor to track Amy who's been kidnapped by Smilers. Finding it abandoned, Liz also tracks the Doctor with it.

Gold plated

Camera

Wireless connection

Star Whale

WHEN EARTH WAS being devastated by solar flares, the planet's nations fled to the stars – except for Britain. Hearing the cries of the country's children, a Star Whale arrived to help them. However the creature's kindness was mistaken for a lucky coincidence and the beast was captured by Britain's leaders. They built a ship upon its back and cruelly forced it to carry the nation through space.

Gentle Giant

Star Whales are giant alien creatures with several flippers and tentacles that trail behind them. They also have numerous tendrils along their chin and undercarriage. Over the years the Star Whale population has declined – in fact the one carrying the Starship UK is the last of its kind.

Driving Force

Builders of Starship UK didn't understand the benevolence of the Star Whale and thought it would only carry them under duress. They accessed the Star Whale's brain and blasted it with energy bolts to make the creature fly faster. This cruel practice has been taking place ever since.

Dinner Time!

After the Doctor presses the "Protest" button in the voting booth, the floor below disappears and he and Amy fall down into the Star Whale's mouth. To escape, the Doctor makes the monster vomit – it's not dignified but it works!

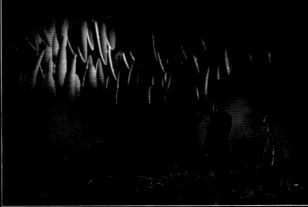

After landing in the monster's mouth the Doctor finally understands how the spaceship flies without an engine.

Democracy

Every five years people over the age of 16 find out the truth about the Starship UK in a film shown to them in voting booths. Afterwards, they are given a choice: to protest about what they have learnt or to forget it. Most choose to forget; those who protest are fed to the beast.

Each massive tower block houses an entire county

Like her subjects, Liz Ten is shown the truth about Starship UK, but every ten years instead of every five. As Queen she must choose to "Forget" or "Abdicate".

Button to renounce throne

Button to forget the truth

At Winder Division 1, Hawthorne and the Winders watch the citizens – and the Queen herself – on huge television monitors.

Star Whale Facts

• Star Whales communicate using sounds that are too high pitched for the human ear.
• According to legend, Star Whales helped the first human space travellers to navigate their way through space safely.
• Star Whales are bioluminescent creatures and have glowing spots on their tentacles and tendrils.

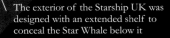

The exterior of the Starship UK was designed with an extended shelf to conceal the Star Whale below it

Friend not foe

In the Tower of London, where the Star Whale is "piloted", Mandy and Timmy see a huge tendril emerge from a hole in the floor. They learn that it is part of the Star Whale. Instead of attacking, it strokes them affectionately. Amy sees this and pieces together the clues: the creature is ancient, kind and hates to see children harmed – it deliberately came to Earth to try to save them and didn't need to be coerced into helping.

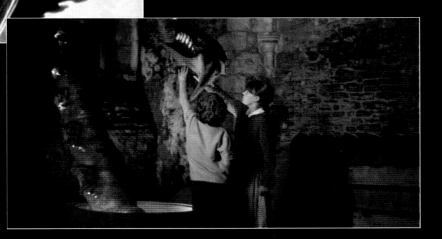

Saturnyns

ONE WOMAN AND THOUSANDS of her male children are the only surviving members of a race of vampire fish fleeing from their planet of Saturnyne. The woman and her oldest son settle in 16th century Venice as humans called Rosanna and Francesco Calvierri. They establish a desirable school for young ladies, the House of Calvierri, and plot to restore their race. Meanwhile Rosanna's other children are lying in wait in the canals.

It would be easy to mistake the Calvierri Girls for vampires with their fangs, aversion to sunlight and the fact that mirrors don't show their reflections. In fact they are worse – Saturnyns. A perception filter manipulates the brainwaves of anyone looking so they see humans. The fangs are still seen because self-preservation overrides the mirage and the human brain gets confused in mirrors, which is why they have no reflection.

The House of Calvierri

Rosanna is a fearsome matriarch who carries the sole responsibility for ensuring the future of her race. She is converting the girls at her school into female Saturnyns. She drinks their human blood and replaces it with her own to make them suitable mates for her male children. Her son Francesco is a ferocious predator with a cruel streak, but he is also fiercely devoted to his mother, which turns out to be a fatal flaw.

ISABELLA

Before joining the House of Calvierri, Isabella's clothes are dowdy and very basic

Saturnyns are amphibious aliens who need constant hydration when on the land. They have four insectoid legs and a thick tail, and with their razor-sharp teeth they feed in swarms like piranha.

Aristocratic Aspirations

Impoverished boat-builder Guido hopes his daughter will gain a better position in society by joining the House of Calvierri. He misses 17-year-old Isabella terribly and when he sees her out walking and she doesn't recognise him, he is convinced that something sinister has happened.

Isabella betrays the Calvierris by helping the Doctor to escape from them. She pays for her treachery with her life – she is fed to the Saturnyns in the canal.

Opulent attire denotes wealth and stature

Smells of fish

FRANCESCO CALVIERRI

ROSANNA
CALVIERRI

Reticella lace ruff
reflects fish quills
of natural form

Alien Technology

Rosanna receives visitors to the palatial House of
Calvierri sitting on a grand throne. It is a symbol of
her opulent life, but the intricate gold work and rich
velvet also hide advanced Saturnyne technology.
The chair is the control hub for a complex system
of circuits that can manipulate the weather.

Calvierri
coat of arms
bears a fish
emblem

Control hub
for elements
manipulator

Orbs open
to reveal
controls

Rosanna parades the Calvierri girls through the streets
of Venice as a way of enticing further girls to join the
auspicious House of Calvierri. The perception filter
ensures that onlookers see them as poised, beautiful
women. However, if they could be seen in their alien
form, Rosanna's school wouldn't be quite so appealing.

CALVIERRI THRONE

ELEMENTS
MANIPULATOR

Rosanna can control the weather
with this elements manipulator,
situated on the spire of the
House of Calvierri. It forms dark
clouds, creates rain and causes the
sky to boil. It can whip up storms
violent enough to trigger
earthquakes and tidal waves that
will swamp Venice.

With a flick of a switch on
a high-speed rotating cog,
the Doctor ends the
storm and saves Venice.

Bending the Heavens

Rosanna uses her influence in Venice
society to seal the city under the pretence
of protecting it from the Plague. She
plans to use the elements manipulator to
sink Venice, kill all its human inhabitants
and create a new Saturnyne colony.

On/off switch
hidden on cog

Wheels and
spheres rotate
around the
central spike

Two halves of orb
close to conceal the
inner workings

Device is disguised as
decorative sphere on
building spire

Perception filter
makes piscine
aliens appear
human

When Rosanna fails to ensure the future of her
race, she jumps into a canal in human form and
is devoured by her children. The Doctor tries
to save her, but she is determined to die.

Silurians

LONG BEFORE HUMANS evolved, the Silurians ruled Earth. When an apocalypse was predicted, the humanoid reptilian race retreated deep underground to hibernate until it was safe to return to the surface. In the meantime, evolution moved on and now human beings believe they own Earth. The Silurians have different ideas, though they themselves are divided.

In the Welsh hamlet of Cwmtaff, a patch of blue grass has led a scientific research team to drill deep into Earth's crust. Since this Discovery Project began, strange things have been happening: bodies vanish from untouched graves, pets go missing and steam pours from holes in the ground.

Family of Fear

Mo Northover works on the Discovery Project. Along with his wife Ambrose and son Elliot, he is astonished to discover the existence of the Silurians. When Ambrose's father is injured by the Silurians and Elliot is kidnapped, they display the worst of human nature and respond with violence. Their fear and anger is born out of love and desperation to protect their family, but it derails the peace process.

Mo helps dyslexic Elliot with his reading every day before work

AMBROSE, MO AND ELLIOT

Battle-scared face

Face has same expressions as a human face

MALOHKEH

ALAYA

Scientist's lab coat

Warrior dress

RESTAC

Martyr

Silurian warriors are woken from hibernation when the drills threaten to destroy their city. Dedicated to ridding Earth of humanity, Alaya is a soldier happy to die for her cause. In fact, she taunts Ambrose into killing her. She believes her murder will trigger a human-Silurian war, enabling her race to reclaim Earth's surface.

Human-like fingers

All clothes hewn from natural underground materials

Aggressor

Restac is Alaya's gene-twin, but as a military commander, she outranks her sister. She is charged with the security of the hibernating population. Some Silurians argue for peace and cohabitation, but Restac has no time for that – she thinks executing the Doctor is a good way to send a message to the "apes".

Clothing denotes high military rank

Cold-Blooded Genius

Malohkeh is a brilliant scientist who has been monitoring changes to life forms on Earth's surface for 300 years while his fellow Silurians sleep. Driven by the quest for scientific discovery, he has no sentimentality towards the creatures he studies and torments, but he doesn't actually intend them any malice.

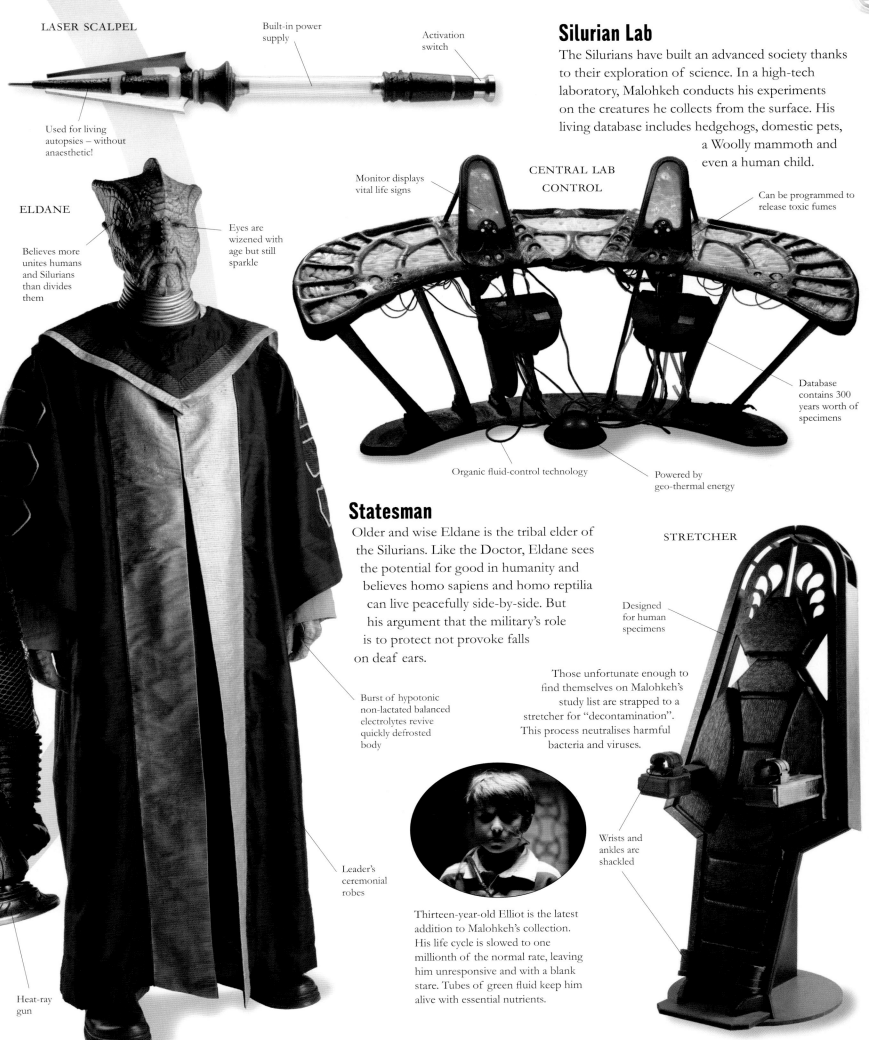

LASER SCALPEL

Built-in power supply

Activation switch

Used for living autopsies – without anaesthetic!

Silurian Lab

The Silurians have built an advanced society thanks to their exploration of science. In a high-tech laboratory, Malohkeh conducts his experiments on the creatures he collects from the surface. His living database includes hedgehogs, domestic pets, a Woolly mammoth and even a human child.

ELDANE

Believes more unites humans and Silurians than divides them

Eyes are wizened with age but still sparkle

Monitor displays vital life signs

CENTRAL LAB CONTROL

Can be programmed to release toxic fumes

Database contains 300 years worth of specimens

Organic fluid-control technology

Powered by geo-thermal energy

Statesman

Older and wise Eldane is the tribal elder of the Silurians. Like the Doctor, Eldane sees the potential for good in humanity and believes homo sapiens and homo reptilia can live peacefully side-by-side. But his argument that the military's role is to protect not provoke falls on deaf ears.

STRETCHER

Designed for human specimens

Those unfortunate enough to find themselves on Malohkeh's study list are strapped to a stretcher for "decontamination". This process neutralises harmful bacteria and viruses.

Burst of hypotonic non-lactated balanced electrolytes revive quickly defrosted body

Leader's ceremonial robes

Wrists and ankles are shackled

Thirteen-year-old Elliot is the latest addition to Malohkeh's collection. His life cycle is slowed to one millionth of the normal rate, leaving him unresponsive and with a blank stare. Tubes of green fluid keep him alive with essential nutrients.

Heat-ray gun

Forked tongue
lashes with enough
power to knock
over a man

Venom glands
take 24 hours
to refill

Chain mail
forged from
underground
metals

Tough ridges of
bone protect
Silurian skull

Body armour
customised to fit
tight to body

Military uniform of the
Silurian warrior caste

Silurian Warriors

THE SILURIANS come from a time when dinosaurs roamed Earth. The need to keep the Silurian cities safe led to the establishment of a warrior caste fiercely protective of its race. For these warriors, nothing is more important than the Silurians' continued survival. Now awake after hibernating for aeons, the warriors are furious that humanity has overrun "their" home. And, just like the primitive apes they regarded as vermin millennia ago, they see humans in the same way.

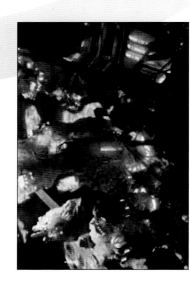

Bathed in an orange glow from the Earth's molten core, the Silurian city spreads majestically over a wide valley. Buildings are hewn from rock and granite sealed together with cooled lava. The settlement has its own self-sufficient ecosystem, processing carbon dioxide and providing food. Geothermal power is used to split water from deep-crust minerals into hydrogen and oxygen, which is stored in pockets above the city for a fresh air supply.

Sisters in Arms

With special training and fearsome armour, Silurian warriors like Restac and Alaya are creatures of precision, beauty and absolute deadliness. With superior Silurian technology, they believe the Silurians can emerge from their underground city and reclaim the surface of Earth. For these soldiers, violence is always the answer.

Heavy boots
needed for tough
underground
terrain

Powerful,
sculptured
muscle tone

HEAT RAY GUN

Molecular
acceleration
barrel

Wide dispersing
heat beam

Safety button

Ornate decoration,
the weapon is also a
piece of art

Silurian Facts

- Silurians are cold-blooded reptiles who bask in the heat from the Earth's molten core.
- They went into hibernation when they thought a planet was going to smash into Earth. This planet, however, went into Earth's orbit and we know it better as the Moon.
- Silurian activity underground releases mineral traces that turn the grass on the surface blue.
  - The creatures have built an ingenious transportation system harnessing geothermal currents that pass through tunnels.

Sun visors shield
eyes used to living
underground

Mask carved to fit
face closely

There's no doubt the humans in Cwmtaff think the Silurian battle mask is terrifying. When the Doctor sees it, however, he quickly recognises the species. Although he's met the Silurians in earlier incarnations, the original rulers of Earth rarely survived the experience.

BATTLE MASK

The Pandorica

THE PANDORICA IS A BOX designed, so the legend goes, as a prison to hold the most feared thing in all the universe; a nameless, terrible monster soaked in the blood of a million galaxies. The Doctor is familiar with the tale, but he never imagined that that description could fit him and that he is the intended inhabitant of the Pandorica box. The Doctor, River and Amy find the Pandorica under Stonehenge. Above it, Roman Britain is flourishing. However, the scenario is actually a trap created by the alien Nestene Consciousness.

The Pandorica has been waiting for the Doctor in an ancient weathered chamber hidden below Stonehenge.

Fake Romans

Above the Pandorica it appears to be Roman Britain, but everything is a fabrication by the Nestene, formed from an imprint of Amy's memories. The Roman Army is the greatest human military machine ever known, but these centurions are not human, let alone Roman.

Hand drops away to reveal Auton gun-stick

Realistic period clothing – but it's all fake!

Information from books that Amy read as a child – about Pandora's Box and Romans – inform the scenario the Nestene create to ensnare the Doctor.

The Pandorica Opens

A gleaming black cube three metres (10 feet) square, the Pandorica is a formidable fortress with layers of security protocols: deadlocks, time-stops, matter lines. But it only takes one scan of the biometric data from the Doctor's handprint for it to start unlocking itself. The Doctor is curious to know what is inside; unaware that it is opening to receive him.

The Auton Deceit

The Roman soldiers are Autons; living plastic in a human shape controlled by the Nestene Consciousness. Soldiers appear human until they glaze over, turn in unison and raise their hands to reveal considerably more firepower than a sword or bow and arrow.

Can shoot or vaporise targets

AUTON GUN-STICK

Jointed fingers solidify when gun activated

The illusion created by the Nestene is convincing with a full Roman encampment near Stonehenge, but a scan of fry particles reveals that energy weapons have been used here.

While the Pandorica opens, time energy is eating up the universe, wiping many races from existence. Some turn to stone, as after-images of creatures that now never existed.

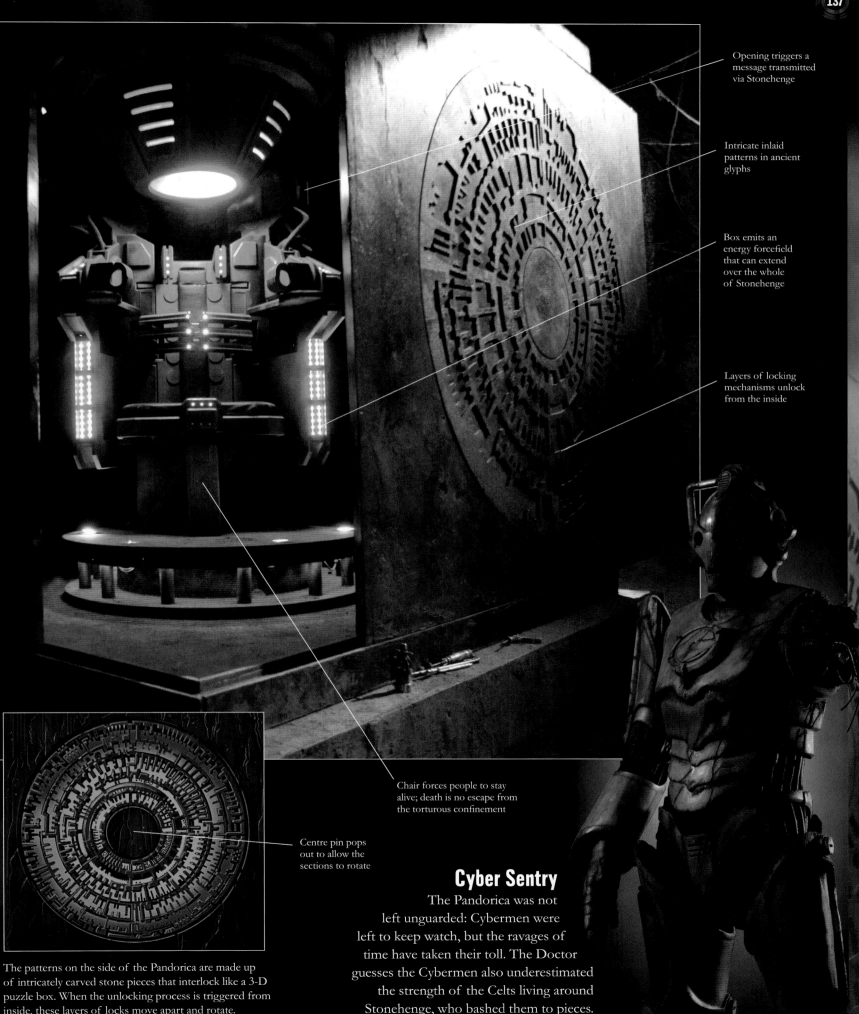

Opening triggers a
message transmitted
via Stonehenge

Intricate inlaid
patterns in ancient
glyphs

Box emits an
energy forcefield
that can extend
over the whole
of Stonehenge

Layers of locking
mechanisms unlock
from the inside

Chair forces people to stay
alive; death is no escape from
the torturous confinement

Centre pin pops
out to allow the
sections to rotate

The patterns on the side of the Pandorica are made up
of intricately carved stone pieces that interlock like a 3-D
puzzle box. When the unlocking process is triggered from
inside, these layers of locks move apart and rotate.

Cyber Sentry

The Pandorica was not
left unguarded: Cybermen were
left to keep watch, but the ravages of
time have taken their toll. The Doctor
guesses the Cybermen also underestimated
the strength of the Celts living around
Stonehenge, who bashed them to pieces.

Enemies

OVER THE CENTURIES, many aliens have crossed swords with the Doctor. Daleks, Cybermen and many other races join in an unlikely alliance to build the Pandorica to put an end to the Doctor once and for all. When the Pandorica opens, they all receive notification from a transmission boosted by Stonehenge. They gather in the skies over Earth in their billions to see the Doctor be locked in the prison.

At first, the Doctor is bemused that the prison is for him. He is astonished that it took such an alliance to entrap him and that he is seen as a great warrior. But when the gravity of the situation becomes clear, he is angry and then remorseful. He feels the pain he has inflicted while saving one species from another.

JUDOON

The Uvodni are a humanoid race with insectoid faces from the Spiral Cluster of the Dragon Nebula

The Cyber Sentry

The Cybermen posted to watch over the Pandorica have stood guard for so long that their organic parts have rotted. However, their metal components are still active and are just as deadly. Although dismembered, their wires spread around the underhenge, searching for fresh meat to replace their decayed organs.

CYBERHEAD

STONE CYBERMAN

The Pandorica chamber also contains petrified Cybermen parts. Time energy seeping from cracks in the Universe have caused the Cybermen to cease to exist, leaving just a stone imprint of their memory.

UVODNI

SONTARAN

Four battle fleets of Sontaran arrive in the skies over Stonehenge

The Cybermen and the Daleks have always been enemies until they join together against the Doctor

CYBERMAN

Roboforms are scavangers who normally accompany other races on invasions

ROBOFORM

SYCORAX

Autons are made of living plastic. These ones have taken on the appearance of Roman soldiers

AUTON

SUPREME DALEK

SILURIAN

A Crooked Smile

The crack in the fabric of time first came to the Doctor's attention in Amelia Pond's bedroom. She had been hearing voices from it and Prisoner Zero used it to escape his Atraxi prison. The Doctor forced it open so it snapped itself shut, but other cracks are getting stronger.

Powerful rays of time energy are pouring from the crack and seeping through the tree-borg forest on board the *Byzantium*, wiping from existence everything in their path.

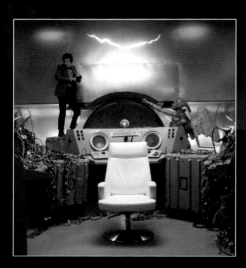

The crack from Amy's bedroom wall was on the *Byzantium* too. An army of Weeping Angels wanted to feed on its energy, but it fed on them, wiping them from history.

Time Energy

O N THE 26TH JUNE 2010, the day of Amy and Rory's wedding, the TARDIS explodes. Because of the Eye of Harmony within it, the temporal energy burns at every point in time and space simultaneously. Cracks begin to appear across the universe. Some are tiny and some are big enough for whole planets to fall through, including Saturnyne, which was home to a race of amphibious vampires. The light pouring out the cracks carries so much temporal power that it wipes from existence anything it touches.

The crack in the universe is caused by the Doctor's TARDIS exploding at every point in time and space

The explosion is triggering total event collapse: every sun will supernova and every moment will never have existed

VINCENT VAN GOGH

Warning from the Past

Artist Vincent van Gogh was misunderstood in his own time, but his visions are invaluable to the Doctor. His brain is open to influence from the transmitter at Stonehenge and he paints what's in his head. His warning of the TARDIS exploding passes through many hands on its way to the Doctor, including Winston Churchill and Liz Ten on Starship UK.

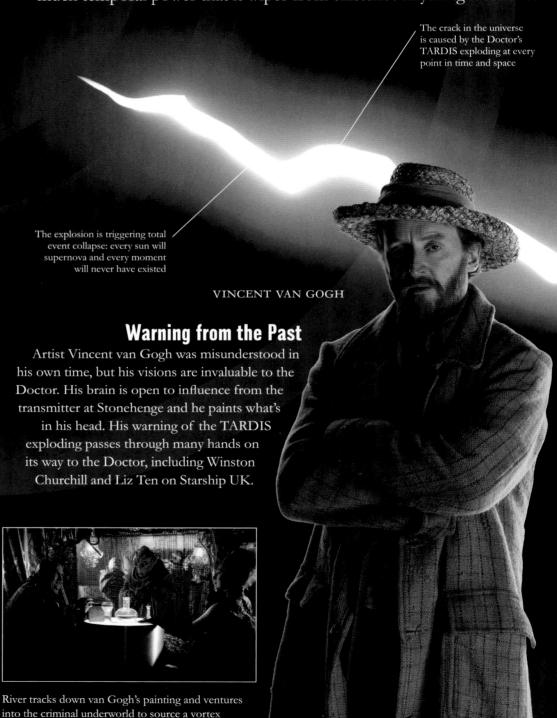

River tracks down van Gogh's painting and ventures into the criminal underworld to source a vortex manipulator to get the painting to the Doctor.

The Anomaly Exhibition

After 2,000 years, the Pandorica turns up at the Anomaly Exhibition, a display of impossible things at the National Museum. Surrounded by myth and legend, it was discovered under Stonehenge in 107 AD and taken back to Rome. Stolen by Goths, and sold by Marco Polo, it was later recovered from the Aegean seabed. During the the World War II Blitz it was rescued from a burning warehouse in London.

STONE DALEK

A blast of Alpha Mezon through the eye-stalk is fatal

Time energy from the Pandorica allows the dormant stone Daleks to come alive

The Dalek-shaped stone is an imprint residue of a Dalek that ceased to exist when it was consumed by energy from the cracks in time and space.

Stone Daleks

Along with the Pandorica, two stone Daleks are also on display at the museum. There, the Doctor catches up with the Pandorica and throws it into the heart of the exploding TARDIS in order to reboot the universe. The temporal power of the TARDIS and the memory of the universe housed within the Pandorica cause a second big bang, resetting the universe and closing the cracks of time energy.

Index

Numbers in bold indicate main entries

A

Abzorbaloff 79
Adherents of the Repeated Meme **76**, 77
Adipose 23, 112
Adipose 3 56, 112
Adipose Industries 22, 112
airship 70
Alaya 27, **132**, 134–135
Ambassadors of the City State of Binding Light 76
anatomy (of Time Lords) 9, **10–11**, 33
Angelo, Father 86
Anomaly Exhibition, the 140 *see also* National Museum, the
antiplastic 22
Aplan Mortarium 23, **64**
Archangel Network 103
ATMOS 117
Atraxi 21, 22, 27, 28, 124, **125**, 140
Autons 27, **136**, 139

B

Baines, Jeremy 100
Bane 38
Bannakaffalatta 111
battles (of)
    Canary Wharf 36, 49, 72
    the Sphere Chamber 49
Beast, the 92, **93**
Black Dalek, the *see* Dalek Sec
Blaine, Margaret 79
Blood, Family of 40, 41, **100–101**, 102
Bowie Base One 9, **121**
Bracewell, Professor Edwin 58, **59**, 61
Britain 58, 59, 128 *see also* Cardiff; England; Leadworth; London; Stonehenge; Wales
Brooke, Captain Adelaide 9, **121**
Byzantium, the 20, 30, 64, 65, 140

C

Caan *see* Dalek Caan
Caecilius family 33, 115
CAL (computer) 120
Calvierri, Francesco **130**, 131
Calvierri, Rosanna 9, 130, **131**
Calypso, Sally 85
Canary Wharf 46 *see also* Battle of Canary Wharf
Cantrell, Suki Macrae 80
Capricorn, Max 110, **111**
Cardiff 16, 32, 36, 88
Carrionites **98–99**
Casp, Matron 84
Cassandra, Lady 76, **77**
catpeople **84–85**
chameleon arch 40, 41
chameleon circuit 15, 16

Chantho 102, **105**
Chip 77
Christie, Agatha 113
Churchill, Winston 9, 25, 58, **59**, 140
clockwork repair robots 90, **91**
Clom 56, 79
Cobb, General 119
Cofelia, Matron 112
Copper, Mr 57, 111
crack in time 27, 28, 64, 124, **140–141** *see also* time energy
Crucible, the 56
Cult of Skaro 43, 47, **50–51**, 52, 53, 56
Cyber Controller 71
Cyberghosts 48
Cyberleader **48**, 49, 72
CyberKing **72–73**
Cybermen 37, **68–69**, 70, 71, 72, 73
    and the Sphere Chamber 47, 48, 49
    and the Pandorica 137, 138, 139
Cybershades **72–73**
Cybus Industries 68, 69, **70–71**

D

Dalek Caan 51, 52, 53, 56
Dalek Emperor 43, 44, 45, 50, 52
Dalek Jast 51, 52, 53
Dalek Sec 47, 49, **50–51**, **52–53**
Dalek Thay 51, 52, 53
Dalekanium 43, 44, 50, 52, 53, 57, 61
Daleks 6, 14, 32, 37, **42–43**, 44–45
    and the Cult of Skaro 50–51
    and Davros 38, 42, 43, 54–55, 56–57
    DNA 52, 53, 60
    and Dalek flagship **44–45**
    and the Genesis Ark 46, 47, 48, 49
    and the Great Time War 6, 43, 44, 50, 51, 56, 108
    as Ironsides 9, **58–59**
    new race of **60–61**
    and the Pandorica 138, 139, 141
    stone Daleks 31, 137, 141
    Supreme Dalek
        (red) 56
        (white) **60–61**, 139
Davros 19, 33, 34, 37, 38, 42, 43, **54–55**, 56–57
Diagoras, Mr 85
Disciples of Light 93
Discovery Project 132–133
DNA
    Dalek 52, 53, 60
    Time Lord 11, 33, 53, 119 *see also* Doctor-Donna, the; human Doctor, the
Doctor-Donna, the **33**, 38, 107
Doctor's daughter, the 9, 119
Doomsday Ghosts *see* Cyberghosts
Dream Lord, the **11**, 16, 29

E

Earth 8, 77, 94, 100
    at Christmas 72, 82, 83, 94, 111
    in danger 6, 43, 58, 61, 72, 78, 79, 88, 104, 105, 106, 107, 109, 114,

116, 122, 124, 125
    parallel Earths 49, 70
    moved to the Medusa Cascade 14, 36, 38, 56, 57
    natural end of 6, 74–75, 84
    and the Silurians 9, 27, 132, 133, 134, 135
    see also Cardiff; Leadworth; London; New York City; Pompeii; Stonehenge; Venice
Eddison, Lady Clemency 113
Editor, the 80, 81
Eknodines 26, **29**
Eldane **133**
elements manipulator 131
Emperor *see* Dalek Emperor, the
Empire State Building 52, **53**
Empress of the Racnoss 94
England 6, 100 *see also* Britain; Leadworth; London; Stonehenge
Eye of Harmony **14**, **16**, 102, 109, 140

F

Face of Boe, the 22, **32**, 76, 85, 102
Family of Blood, the 40, 41, **100–101**, 102
Farisi, Rosita 73
Farringham School 40, 41, **100**
Final Experiment, the 52, 53
Finnegan, Florence 95
Fire Trap, the (asteroid) 82
flagship (Dalek) **44–45**
Flood, the **121**
fob watch 40, 41, 102, 103
Foster, Miss 112
Frame, Alonso 32, 110
Futurekind 105

G

Gadget 121
Gallifrey 1, 6, 15, 16, 38, 39, 43, 108, **109**
Gelth, the 6, **88**
Genesis Ark, the **46**, 47, 48, 49, 50, 51
Globe Theatre 99
Golightly, Reverend 113
gravity globe 23
Great Britain 58, 59, 128 *see also* Cardiff; England; Leadworth; London; Stonehenge; Wales
Great Time War, the 6, 43, 44, 46, 47, 50, 51, 54, 56, 102, **108**, 109
Great War, the (1914–1918) 40
Gwyneth 88

H

Halpen family 66
Halpen, Mr **66**, 67
Hame, Novice 85
Hardaker, Captain 110
Harkness, Jack 10, 12, 31, **32**, 36, 38, 56, 57
Hartigan, Mercy 73
Hath, the **118–119**
Heavenly Host **110–111**

High Council *see* Time Lord High Council
Hop Pyleen Brothers 76
hospital
    Leadworth Hospital 27, 28, 124, 125
    Royal Hope Hospital 35, 95
Home Box 30
House of Calvierri, the 130, 131
human/Dalek hybrid 52, **53**
human Doctor, the **11**, 34, 57
Huon energy 18, 94

I

Immortality Gate, the **106**, 107
infosphere 80
infospike 80
infostamp 73
Ironsides **58–59**
Isabella 130

J

Jabe Ceth Ceth Jafe 75
Jagrafress, the 80, 81
Jast *see* Dalek Jast
Jenny (the Doctor's daughter) 9, **119**
Jones, Harriet 57
Jones, Martha 12, **35**, 37, 41, 52, 57, 62, 84, 99, 100, 101, 102, 103, 119
Judoon 35, 57, 83, 95, **96–97**, 138

K

K-9 38, **39**
Kaleds 42, 54
Krafayis 23
Krillitanes 39, **89**

L

Lake, Jackson 73
Lammersteen scanner 22
laser screwdriver 102, 103
Latimer, Tim 101
Leadworth 24, 26, **28–29**
Leadworth Hospital 27, 28, 124, 125
Lethbridge-Stewart, Brigadier 37
Library, the 20, 31, **120**
Liz Ten **127**, 129, 140
Llewellyn, Daniel 82
London 6, 8, 36, 46, 47, 70, 71, 72, 73, 94, 111, 112, 122
    Blitz 27, 58, 141
Lucius Petrus Dextrus 115
Lumic, John 68, **70**, 71
lupine wavelength haemovariform **86–87**
Lux, Charlotte Abigail 120
Lux, Felman 120

M

Mace, Colonel 37, 117
MacNannovich, Cal "Sparkplug" 76
Macra 85
magna-clamp 23
Malcassairo 102, 105
Malokeh **132**, 133
Marius, Professor 39

Mars 121
Master, the 6, 11, 12, 35, **102-103**, 104, 105, 106, 107, 109
Maze of the Dead 23, **64**
Medusa Cascade, the 14, 38, **56**
Messaline 9, 118, 119
MI5 79
Moon, the 97, 135
Mortarium 23, **64**
Motorway, the 85
Mott, Wilfred 12, 13, **33**, 107, 111
Moxx of Balhoon 76

N

Naismith, Abigail 107
Naismith, Joshua 106, **107**
National Museum, the 31, 140, 141
Nestene Consciousness, the 6, 22, 136
Nestene duplicates 27, 139
New Earth 32, **84–85**
New New York 84, 85
New York City 52, 53
Nightingale, Kathy **62**, 63
Nightingale, Larry 63
Noble, Donna 11, 12, **33**, 38, 94, 107, 115, 119
Noble, Sylvia **33**
Northover, Ambrose **132**
Northover, Elliot **132**, 133
Northover, Mo **132**

O

Oblivion Continuum 59, 61
Octavian, Father **64**, 65
Ood 7, 13, **66–67**, 92
Ood Operations 2, 3, 22, 66, 67
Ood Sigma 66–67
Ood-Sphere 66
Osterhagen Key 37
Other Doctor, the 73

PQ

Pakoo Mr and Mrs 76
Pandorica, the 27, **136–137**, 138–139, 141
Paradox Machine **104**, 105
pathogenesis detector 23
perception filter 40, 102, 130, 131
Peth, Astrid 111
Plasmavores **95**, 97
Platform One **74–75**, 76–77, 84
Pompadour, Madame de 90, **91**
Pompeii 16, 33, **114–115**
Pond, Amelia 13, 16, 24, **25**, 28, 124, 125, 140 *see also* Pond, Amy
Pond, Amy 11, 19, 23, **24–25**, 26, 27, 28, 29, 61, 64, 65, 124, 125, 128, 129, 136 *see also* Pond, Amelia
poppets 99
Prisoner Zero 21, 27, 28, **124–125**, 140
progenitor device **60**, 61
Project Indigo 37
psychic paper 22, 74, 86
psychic pollen 11, 16
Pyroviles **114–115**
Pyrovillia 56, 114
Queen, the 111

Liz Ten **127**, 129, 140
Victoria 9, 36, 86, 87

R

Racnoss 33, **94**
Rassilon 3, **107**, 108, 109
Rattigan, Luke 116, **117**
Raxacoricofallapatorians 78, 79
Raxacoricofallapatorius 78, 79
Reality Bomb, the 19, 33, **56**, 57
Redfern, Joan 41
regeneration 8, 11, **12–13**
Reinette 90, **91**
repair robots 90, **91**
Restac **132**, 134–135
Rift, the 16, 32, 36, 46, **88**
Roboform 139
robots
    clockwork repair 90, **91**
    Gadget **121**
    K-9 38, **39**
    Smilers **126–127**
    spiders **76**, 77
    Winders **127**
    see also Autons
Royal Hope Hospital 35, 95
Rutans 116
Ryder, Dr 67

S

San Helios 122–123
Sanchez, General 37
Sanctuary Base 92, 93
Satellite 5 32, **80–81**
Saturnyne 130, 131, 140
Saturnyns 2, 6, 9, **130–131**, 144
Saxon, Harold 36, 37, **103**, 106
    see also Master, the
Saxon, Lucy **103**, 106
Scarecrow Soldiers 100, **101**
Scott, Ida 93
screwdriver
    laser 102, 103
    sonic 1, 3, **20–21**, 30, 31, 48, 49, 125
Sec *see* Dalek Sec
Shadow Proclamation **57**, 96, 125
Shakespeare, William 98, 99
Shipton, Billy 63
Sibyls/Sibylline Sisterhood 115
signet ring **103**, 106
Silurians 9, 11, 27, **132–133**, **134–135**, 139
Singh, Dr 67
Sisters of Plenitude 84
Skaro 42, 43, 51, 54
Skaro, Cult of 43, 47, **50–51**, 52, 53, 56
Skasas Paradigm 89
Skorr, Commander 117
Slitheen **78–79**
Smilers **126–127**
Smith, John **40–41**
Smith, Luke 38
Smith, Mickey **34**, 47, 49, 90, 91
Smith, Mr (computer) **38**, 57
Smith, Sarah Jane 12, **38**, 39, 57
Song, River 19, 20, 22, 23, **30–31**, 64,

120, 136, 140
sonic screwdriver 1, 3, **20–21**, 48, 49, 125
    River Song's 20, 30, 31
    see also laser screwdriver
Sontar 116
Sontarans 35, 37, **116–117**, 138
Source, the 118, **119**
Souza, Lady Christina de **122**, 123
Sparrow, Sally 62, 63
Sphere Chamber, the **46**, 47, 48, 49
spider robots **76**, 77
SS *Madame de Pompadour* **90–91**
St Catherine's Glen Monastery 86
Staal, General **116**
Star Whale 24, **128–129**
Starship UK 24, **126–127**, **128–129**, 140
Steward, the 74, 77
Street, Peter 99
Stingrays 122, **123**
Sto 110, 111
Stoker, Mr 95
stone Daleks 31, 137, 141
Stonehenge 136, 137, 138, 140, 141
Subwave Network 57
Sun, the 6, **74–75**
Supreme Dalek
    (red) 56
    (white) **60–61**, 139
Sycorax 10, 33, **82–83**, 139

T

TARDIS 6–7, 8, 12, **14–15**, **16–19**, 25, 30, 31, 40, 45, 74, 81, 100, 102, 121
    explosion of 140–141
    machinery 11, 16–19, 22, 23, 40–41
    power for 10, 63
    and the time vortex 32, 44
    towing Earth 19, 38
Taylor, Doctor Malcolm 123
teleports 37, 79, 111
temporal energy 27, 138, **140–141** *see also* crack in time
Thals 42, 43
Thay *see* Dalek Thay
Time Agency 32
time energy 27, 138, **140–141** *see also* crack in time
Time Lord(s) 8, 9, 108, 109
    anatomy of 9, **10–11**, 33
    DNA 11, 33, 53, 119 *see also* Doctor-Donna, the; human Doctor
    High Council 12, 107, **108–109**
    and Great Time War 6, 44, 46, 108, 109
    regeneration 8, 11, **12–13**
    science and technology 14, 15, 16–19, 20–21, 22–23, 40–41, 46, 47, 102, 104
    see also Master, the; Rassilon
time vortex 6–7, 32, 34, 44
Time War *see* Great Time War, the
Titanic
    (space craft) 32, **110**, 111

(ship) 8
Toclafane **104–105**
Torchwood
    Institute 6, 32, **36**, 37, 46, 47, 48, 49, 87
    House 86, 87
tribophysical waveform macro-kinetic extrapolator 23
Trickster 33, 38
Trickster's beetle 33
Tritovores 123
Tyler, Jackie **34**, 79
Tyler, Rose 12, 13, 16, 19, 23, 32, **34**, 43, 44, 47, 48, 49, 74, 75, 77, 84, 86, 90, 91

U

Ultimate Sanction, the 108, **109**
United Intelligence Taskforce (UNIT) 6, 35, **37**, 117, 123
Untempered Schism 102
Utopia 102, 105
Uvodni 138

V

Valiant, the 37
vampires 130, 131 *see also* Saturnyns
van Gogh, Vincent 16, 23, 25, 140
Vashta Nerada **120**
Venice 9, 26, 27, 130, **131**
Vespiform **113**
Vesuvius, Mount 114, 115
Victoria, Queen 9, 36, 86, 87
Vinvocci 106, 111
Visionary, the 108
visual recognition device 23
Void, the 23, 49
Void Ship **46**, 47, 48, 49, 50
vortex *see* time vortex
vortex manipulator 32, 100, 140

W

Wales 132 *see also* Britain; Cardiff
warp star 2, 38
Webstar 94
Weeping Angels 20, 23, 25, 30, **62–63**, **64–65**, 140
Werewolf, the 20, **86–87**
Wester Drumlins 62, 63
Williams, Rory 11, 24, **26–27**, 28, 29, 124, 125
Winders **127**
World War I 40
World War II 9, 27, 58, 59, 141

YZ

Yana, Professor 32, 36, 102, 105 *see also* Master, the
zeppelin 70
Zocci 111

LONDON, NEW YORK, MUNICH,
MELBOURNE AND DELHI

SENIOR EDITOR Elizabeth Dowsett
SENIOR DESIGNERS Guy Harvey and Toby Truphet
MANAGING EDITOR Catherine Saunders
PUBLISHING MANAGER Simon Beecroft
CATEGORY PUBLISHER Alex Allan
PRODUCTION EDITOR Sean Daly
PRODUCTION CONTROLLER Nick Seston

First published in Great Britain in 2010 by
Dorling Kindersley Limited,
80 Strand, London, WC2R 0RL

Some content taken from *Doctor Who The Visual
Dictionary*, first published in Great Britain in 2007

2 4 6 8 10 9 7 5 3 1
176212 – 07/10

BBC, DOCTOR WHO (word marks, logos and devices), TARDIS,
DALEKS, CYBERMAN and K-9 (word marks and devices) are
trade marks of the British Broadcasting Corporation and are used
under licence.

BBC logo © BBC 1996. Doctor Who logo © BBC 2009. TARDIS
image © BBC 1963. Dalek image © BBC/Terry Nation 1963.
Cyberman image © BBC/Kit Pedler/Gerry Davis 1966. K-9 image
© BBC/Bob Baker/Dave Martin 1977.

Page Design Copyright © 2010 Dorling Kindersley Limited
A Penguin Company

All rights reserved. No part of this publication may
be reproduced, stored in a retrieval system, or transmitted
in any form or by any means, electronic, mechanical,
photocopying, recording, or otherwise, without the prior
written permission of the copyright owner.

A CIP catalogue record for this book is available from
the British Library.

ISBN: 978-1-40535-033-4

Colour reproduction by Media Development and Printing in the UK
Printed and bound in China by Leo Paper Products Ltd

Artworks: The TARDIS (pages 6–7) by Lee Binding; Sonic
Screwdrivers (pages 20–21) by Peter McKinstry; Leadworth Map
(pages 28–29) by James Southall; Dalek Flagship by John Maloney
(pages 44–45); The Satan Pit by Richard Bonson (page 93);
Pandorica Panel (page 137) by Peter McKinstry.

Dorling Kindersley would like to thank Gary Russell, David Turbitt and Kate Walsh at the BBC; Neil Corry,
Jacqueline Rayner, Andrew Darling, Kerrie Dougherty and David John for their writing; Lindsay Kent and
Lisa Stock for their editorial work and Chris Glynn at the Cardiff School of Art and Design.

Discover more at
www.dk.com

SATURNYNE

Amphibious arthropod
from the planet
Saturnyne

Respiratory
system can both
breathe air and
extract oxygen
from water

Scales overlap
downwards to
reduce drag in
the water

Razor-sharp
teeth for tearing
through flesh

Unlike Earth's insects,
legs sprout from the
abdomen, not
the thorax

Crustaceous
exoskeleton
moults as the
creature grows

Multi-jointed legs end
in bladelike bones that
pierce prey

When on land, body needs
constant hydration

Broad tail helps
keep heavy body
stable on land